M000093165

STEP INTO YOUR BRILLIANCE

REBECCA HALL GRUYTER, COMPILER
#1 INTERNATIONAL BEST SELLING AUTHOR

Published 2019

Printed in the United States of America

Print ISBN: 978-1-7328885-3-1
Publisher Information:

RHG Media Productions

25495 Southwick Drive #103

Hayward, CA 94544

www.YourPurposeDrivenPractice.com

ACKNOWLEDGMENTS

When writing an anthology, it takes many voices willing to join together to bring forth the book in a powerful and united way. It has been such an honor and privilege to work with this amazing group of contributors. I want to thank each of these heart-centered, gifted experts for entrusting us to bring forth and share their powerful chapters.

I want to thank my husband for always cheering me on and encouraging me to SHINE! I thank God for giving me opportunities, opening doors, and bringing together the right people for this powerful project. I thank my parents for their love and support, and my grandmothers for planting the legacy seeds to always choose to Bloom Where You Are Planted, Step Forward, and SHINE!

Contents

FOREWORD

"STEP INTO YOUR BRILLIANCE"
BY REBECCA HALL GRUYTER

Welcome to this powerful anthology! 14 authors, myself included, have made a commitment to authentically share our stories and wisdom to empower and encourage YOU. Thank you for taking this opportunity to ***step into your brilliance,*** which the world is waiting to see!

In these pages you'll receive the life journeys, wisdom, and practical tips that each of us have experienced on our own paths so that you can take action to move forward in the areas that matter most to you in both a practical and profound way.

I'm honored to bring this powerful book to you; it is my vision to support you on your own journey to SHINE in your brilliance, no matter what you may be called to do or what experience you may choose to have in your work or personal life. I believe life is not a solo journey. By coming together, our goal is to encourage and equip you to step further into your gifts, talents, and abilities. Together, as we lift each other up, we are all able to grow, reach more people, and have a greater impact than we do trying to do everything on our own.

I believe this book is a living and interactive 'conversation' speaking wisdom and encouragement into your life. I want to invite you to pause, take a deep breath, and be ready to receive these powerful chapters so they can ignite a fire in you, inspire courage in you, and bring you the focus to step fully into the BRILLIANCE you are being called to step into.

As you go through these chapters, you'll experience authentic and powerful stories of struggle and triumph, of challenges that were not only met but also triumphed over, lifting the person up to even greater things than he or she ever could have imagined! Our authors are individuals just like you, with fears, past stories, and that 'something' inside that calls us to expand, explore, and seek meaning and purpose to our lives.

Where do you feel you might be blocked in stepping into your own brilliance?

"I couldn't believe the energy surrounding me in this enormous hall... thousands of women gathering together. The crowd. The noise. The connection. The moment I was swept up in the crowd and pulled forward. Eventually finding my seat high in the bleachers. A hush falls over the sea of faces. House lights turn down and the stage lights turn on. The event is about to begin... I'm 19 years old and attending my first Women's of Faith Conference, an event that would change my life, plant a seed in my heart, and show me a calling in my life to step forward and SHINE!"

This starts my chapter in this book, when I said "no" to stepping into my brilliance! I had so many reasons for staying stuck in my past, choosing "no," giving in to my fears. Yet, here I am today, loving my life more than ever, using my gifts–my own brilliance–to help millions of people to be seen, heard, and SHINE!

In creating this book, I asked each gifted, open-hearted expert to share his or her stories and wisdom. I'm so proud of what each co-author brought to this book, and I'm honored to have them leaning in to support you. It is my vision and hope that every story and message will touch your heart in some way because we all need others to encourage us, to speak wisdom and truth into us, to love us and cheer us on, and to help us stand up again when we fall. This book will walk beside you to help you run and not grow weary, to complete all that you are called to complete, and to live on purpose and with great purpose while stepping more fully and powerfully into your calling and brilliance.

I am equally honored that you have said "yes" to our book and are entrusting us to support you on your journey.

Stories, inspiration, and motivation are wonderful gifts to our lives! And one of the biggest things I see holding people back is that they "don't know how." This book is designed to help you with the how.

As these authors have tapped into our collective wisdom and expertise, we will help you discover the how and help you to move forward toward what truly matters to you, what you are called to bring forth to your life and to the world. The lives, journeys, wisdom and action steps that these authors bring to you from their hearts are yours to receive–and act on.

Now it's your turn. Are you going to lean in and learn from the wisdom within this book? Will you let us walk beside you on your journey of life? We want to lift you up, support you, encourage, and empower you. It is your choice. You can choose to open the pages and let them pour into you, or you can put this book on a shelf. My heart and prayer are that you will say "yes" to you and lean into the powerful messages that are waiting to pour into you, your heart, and your life.

Here is how to get the most out of this powerful book. The book is divided it three sections, each one designed to meet you exactly where you are at and to support you powerfully. The first section is **Discover Your Brilliance,** the second section is **Claim Your Brilliance,** and our third section is **Step Into Your Brilliance and SHINE!** You can go directly to the section and chapter that speaks to you most powerfully, or start at the beginning and enjoy the flow from start to finish as you take the journey of discovering your brilliance, claiming it, and then fully stepping into it and sharing your brilliance out in the world! At the end of each powerful chapter you will find the author's bio and contact information. I encourage you to "friend" and follow those authors with whom you feel a powerful resonance and connection so that they can continue to pour into and support you on your journey in life.

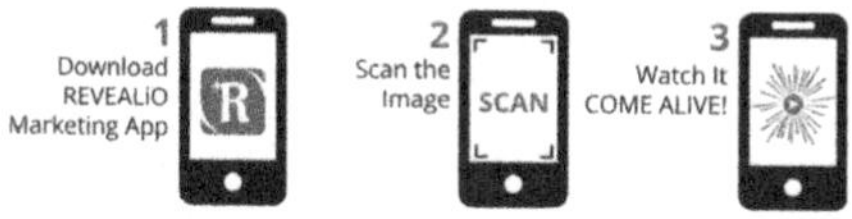

****Special Augmented Reality Print Book Feature**** We are excited to share that we have added the powerful, cutting-edge REVEALiO technology to the print version of our book. You can download the free app, and then once it's loaded on your smart device, it will help the book cover and chapters come alive. Simply open the app and place the window over the cover of the book, and a video message from us will start to play. Some of the authors in this book have also added a special video message to you, too. So make sure to open the app and use it in the beginning of each chapter (putting the picture and title of the author's chapter in the screen box), and those who have saved a video message for you, it will immediately start playing. Enjoy this special feature and personal messages from our powerful authors.

Now the next step is yours. Drink in the stories, insights, and wisdom that are within these pages to serve, support, and inspire you. Take the time to pause, read, and reflect. Listen to the powerful messages of hope that are waiting for you within these transformational and dynamic pages. It's not an accident that you purchased this book and are opening it to read. I invite you to lean in and truly receive the messages and wisdom that will speak to your heart and soul. Enjoy this rich collection of wisdom, insight, and encouragement being provided by our amazing group of experts and influencers. We can't wait to see you STEP INTO YOUR BRILLIANCE!

-----Rebecca Hall Gruyter, Book Compiler
Founder/Owner of Your Purpose Driven Practice and CEO of RHG Media Productions

Rebecca Hall Gruyter

Rebecca Hall Gruyter is an Influencer and Empowerment Leader committed to bringing Experts and Influencers forward so that together we can lean in and make the world a better place one heart and life at a time. She is the owner of *Your Purpose Driven Practice*, creator of the *Women's Empowerment Series* events/TV show, the *Speaker Talent Search*™, and *Your Success Formula*™. Rebecca is an in-demand speaker, an expert money coach, and a frequent guest expert on success panels, tele-summits, TV, and radio shows. Rebecca specializes in using her over 10 million promotional reach to help you be seen, heard, and SHINE!

As the CEO of RHG *Media Productions*™, Rebecca launched the international TV Network (www.RHGTVNetwork.com) to bring even more positive and transformational programming to the world. In July 2017, she launched the Global RHG Magazine & TV Guide, bringing inspirational influences to the world and their messages! In January 2018, she expanded RHG Publishing to now help individual authors bring their books forward as bestsellers so they can be positioned as they bring their powerful book forward.

Rebecca is a popular and syndicated radio talk show host, #1 bestselling author (multiple times), and publisher who wants to help YOU impact the world powerfully!

(925) 787-1572
Rebecca@YourPurposeDrivenPractice.com
www.facebook.com/rhallgruyter (Facebook)
www.YourPurposeDrivenPractice.com (Main Website)
www.RHGTVNetwork.com (TV Network)
www.SpeakerTalentSearch.com (Free Opportunity for Speakers to get on More Stages)
www.EmpoweringWomenTransformingLives.com (Weekly Radio Show)
www.MeetWithRebecca.com (Calendar link to schedule a time to talk with Rebecca)

SECTION 1:

Discover Your Brilliance

WHEN ORDINARY IS NOT AN OPTION
BY MICHELLE CALLOWAY

"I think it is possible for ordinary people to choose to be extraordinary." –Elon Musk

Answering the Call

"It was in that moment that I knew why I was called to build this technology company. Human relationships are what matters most to me in life, and my goal is to enhance them even further through the magical power of technology."
–Michelle Calloway, Founder and CEO of REVEALiO – Augmented Reality Innovative Software Solutions

Have you ever felt that nudge in your gut that won't leave you alone, or that sense of longing that keeps you up at night? What about that voice in your head that keeps getting louder and louder? If you are, there's a strong chance you're being called to do something with it.

"I believe there's a calling for all of us. I know that every human being has value and purpose. The real work of our lives is to become aware. And awakened. To answer the call." —Oprah Winfrey

My calling came in the form of an unconscious obsession. In 2012, when I owned my graphic design agency, I was introduced to a new technology called augmented reality. It was fresh, edgy, and incredibly exciting! Augmented reality (AR) technology bridges our physical world with virtual content such as 3D graphics, video overlays, real time data, etc. You are able to see and interact with the virtual content when you view it through a smart lens, such as a smart phone or smart glasses.

As you can imagine, I was pretty excited about this new technology that offered another level of communication and connection. I'd never seen anything like it. This was a whole new level of excitement all together. I literally couldn't sleep for TWO WHOLE WEEKS! I tried desperately to focus on other things; it was as if someone else was in control of my mind.

Only once I succumbed (to this calling), and acknowledged that I was being chosen to do something with it, did I experience rest from the intensity of thought. It was quite an overwhelming experience. When something grabs a hold of you like that and won't let go, you know you are meant to do something with it. Chances are, it's bigger than you. Most callings are. The important question is, are you going to accept the call and fulfill your purpose through it?

"If you find what you do each day seems to have no link to any higher purpose, you probably want to rethink what you're doing." —Ronald Heifetz, *The Practice of Adaptive Leadership: Tools and Tactics for Changing Your Organization and the World*

Finding Purpose and Passion

Have you heard the phrase, "if you love what you do, it doesn't feel like work?" Along those same lines, if you are answering the call that has been placed on your life, then it will feel so worthwhile and purposeful that it won't feel like work. There is no greater purpose in life than to be fulfilling your destiny.

"If you have a strong purpose in life, you don't have to be pushed. Your passion will drive you there." – Roy T. Bennett, *The Light in the Heart*

Sometimes you don't understand why you were called to do what you were called to do. That's okay, because oftentimes it's bigger than you, and you may not ever be able to understand it. The important thing is that you believe there is a purpose to your calling and that you will be rewarded somehow for accepting the call and doing the work required.

When I first accepted the call to build an augmented reality (AR) technology company, I didn't understand why I was doing it, or what I was building exactly. I just threw myself into learning all that I could in hopes that someday it would be revealed to me why I was personally called to do this.

Luckily it was only a couple of months into developing my first prototype that I was blessed to learn why I was the one called to develop this new technology. The revelation happened one day when a young friend of mine came over to my office. She knew that I could make objects and images magically COME ALIVE with virtual content. She had fallen in love with a young man who was deployed overseas in the military, and she missed him like crazy. She asked if I could help her create a greeting card that would allow him to hear her and see her anytime he wanted. I got goosebumps all over my body, and I excitedly agreed to help her create this very special card.

When he received the printed card with her beautiful face on it, he was very moved. But, when he viewed the card through the mobile app and she started talking to him on the card, he said it rocked him to his core! He felt that she was literally right there with him! He carried the card in his wallet everyday while serving overseas because he felt that she was somehow embodied in the card.

It was in that moment that I knew why I was called to build this technology company. Having lost my soulmate way too prematurely in life, I truly understand the value of human relationships. It is now my duty, honor, and privilege to answer this calling to make these amazing interactive experiences possible for everyone, no matter their age or their budget.

"The purpose of life is not to be happy. It is to be useful, to be honorable, to be compassionate, to have it make some difference that you have lived and lived well." —Ralph Waldo Emerson

Don't Go It Alone

"He who has a why to live for can bear almost any how."
—Friedrich Nietzsche

When I first answered the call to build this AR technology company, I was frustrated because I knew nothing about it. I had no prior training in developing technology, and up until the soldier story, I didn't even understand why, or what, I was building.

Once I gained clarity on the purpose behind my calling, the passion quickly took over, and my appetite to learn was insatiable. I begged the person who originally showed me the technology to teach me everything he knew. I also sought knowledge from successful business professionals on how I should set up the business.

"If you want the answer—ask the question."
—Lori Myers, *Make it Happen*; *A Healthy, Competitive Approach to Achieving Personal Success*

Maybe you are being called to step into a realm that you have no prior experience in. Just because it's your calling doesn't mean you have to go it alone. I recommended that you seek help, guidance, and counsel from industry experts as you embark upon the unknown. In fact, I think it blesses others to have them join you and support you on your journey to fulfill your calling. Even Steve Jobs had his Wozniak.

Finding the right people to join you on your journey may happen quickly or it may take some time. Either way, try to be open to what comes your way, but also be cautious and do your due diligence by vetting people before asking them to join your innermost circle of trust.

Fortitude

"*Action is the foundational key to all success.*" –Pablo Picasso

Years into answering the call, I had a preconceived idea that if I build it, they will come, just like in the movie *Field of Dreams*. It didn't exactly happen like that for me. My first mobile app project was an augmented reality greeting card app. I pursued this creative direction as a response to the soldier story I mentioned earlier. I felt that enhancing human connection through interactive greeting cards was a wonderful answer to the call.

My team and I began demonstrating the technology at wedding fairs, because brides and grooms could easily use this tool to enhance their connection with loved ones via interactive wedding announcements, thank you cards, etc. I was expecting a surge of purchases from our outreach efforts, but instead I mostly received feedback. The feedback was useful, but I was rather disappointed in the lack of revenue we generated over a six-month period after launching the Greetings app.

My takeaway from the wedding fair feedback was that there was desire and need for these types of interactive branded experiences in the business world. Business owners need to enhance their connections with people, too. So, we set out to build an AR Marketing app that would benefit business owners. This new app gave business owners a way to uniquely differentiate themselves when meeting people in person, whether networking or at a tradeshow.

Again, I expected that if I built it, they would come. This new B2B marketing app generated quite a bit of interest, but it became clear that there was still work to be done. I needed to learn how to market this new app and how to close more sales. My background was in digital media creation and mobile app development, not the psychology of marketing and sales. Back to school I went, this time signing up to join mastermind groups that focused on these two topics. I spent an entire year learning how to focus our messaging on benefits versus functionality, how to create desire and demand, and how to make an irresistible offer.

When you find yourself in uncharted waters in response to your calling, try reaching out to other captains who have already sailed those waters successfully. Find yourself a mentor in each aspect of what you are doing so that you can glean from them and avoid making the same mistakes they made along the way.

You may feel unsettled at times, and that's okay; you are outside of your comfort zone, and that's where amazing things happen. Fear may try to sneak its ugly head into your situation, but belief in your purpose and mission will overcome it every time. Stay focused on the end goal, which is fulfilling your purpose, and don't give up until you've reached the finish line.

"The secret is not following the right path, it's following that right path to the end. Don't quit, my friend, until you've arrived."
—Toni Sorenson

I have wanted to give up many times on this journey. Sometimes the work gets too hard and I grow weary. When I pull outside of that moment and look at the bigger picture, I am reminded that I was called to do this, and there is a higher purpose to what I'm doing. This fresh perspective recharges my battery and I keep going.

"We focus on the reasons why we 'can't' at the expense of the far greater reasons why we 'can'."
—Craig D. Lounsbrough, *The Eighth Page*

Hopefully, you have a good support group of friends and family who believe in you and what you are doing. If not, try meeting fellow, like-minded people at networking events, and begin building supportive new relationships.

Many of the people that have reshaped history did so by stepping out and doing something extraordinary. They probably answered a call that was placed on their lives. It's usually not an easy path, but I believe it will be rewarding beyond anything we've ever known. To live life with purpose will ultimately make a difference in your life and in others'. Whether you get to experience what that difference is/was in your lifetime is irrelevant. The important thing is, you lived your life brilliantly! Well done.

Tips To Answering Your Brilliant Calling:

1. Recognize the call.
2. Answer the call with a YES!
3. Find your purpose, passion, and why.
4. Don't go it alone, bring in the help and support that you need.
5. KEEP GOING. See your calling ALL the way through. Be willing to bring it fully forward.

Michelle Calloway

Michelle Calloway is a speaker, int'l bestselling author, tech founder and CEO of REVEALiO Inc., an innovative software solutions company, and Founder of the Tech With Heart Network, an online community and TV show empowering small business success in a rapidly changing digital era.

She is driven to success in response to a calling she believes has been placed on her life. Her goal is to make augmented reality interactive experiences accessible and affordable for everyone, to enhance human connection, and to empower business owners to have more impact, influence, and income.

Michelle has been featured in *Inc.* magazine and praised by Kevin Harrington, Innovator and Creator of the Infomercial, and Original Shark on ABC's hit TV Show, *Shark Tank*, for providing small business owners with a unique differentiator that creates organic conversions.

Calloway combines her expertise in visual communication with the emerging world of augmented reality (AR) technology. Augmented reality technology overlays virtual content on top of real-world objects or images when they are viewed through a mobile or wearable smart device.

Michelle wants to share her inspirational story as a thought-leader and teach the power of interactive branded experiences to forward-thinking business owners and corporate leaders. Her heart is to empower small businesses to gain the ultimate competitive advantage in an Amazon era by captivating their audiences and influencing their buying decisions.

Email: mcalloway@revealio.com
Websites:
https://michellecalloway.us
https://revealio.com
https://techwithheartnetwork.com

BRILLIANT RELATIONSHIP WITH YOU!

BY SONIA FERRELL

Are you making progress in areas where you wish to contribute, create, and experience? If so, that is great! If not, ask yourself this question; when do you feel the most energized and powerful in your life? Is it in your job, with your friends, as a parent, or in the garden? Is it when you are resourceful, part of a community, being of service to clients, or somewhere completely different? Wherever it is, this is where your brilliance lives. **This is where your brilliance lives; this is the powerful, resourceful You!**

For years, I ignored my deep desires to create powerful contributions with transformative leadership work. I love the work of creating value for others, but I held myself back. My excuse was I didn't have time; I was too busy. The reality was I didn't have a clear direction or path I could follow. I didn't have a mentor or coach to guide me toward the necessary steps to reach my goal. I continued living the fast-paced professional life where responsibility increased with promotions. My duties keep increasing: I became a wife, a cook, a housewife in a sense, and a new mom. I struggled to manage it all. I was sinking, letting life happen to me. I was told several times "slow down and smell the roses." I thought, "I have too many things to do," and all I knew was doing, doing it all and more. Until a life event stopped me completely.

One day the tension in my neck and shoulders got worse, triggering headaches. The first thing that came to my mind was to get a chiropractor's adjustment. This had worked in the past, so I went during my work break. That afternoon I got home and finished packing for a two-week family vacation trip, which was exciting! Exactly a week after seeing the chiropractor and into our family vacation, the headaches returned (mild), and the next morning I was hospitalized.

That morning, I was awakened by my two-year-old daughter around six-thirty. I felt nauseous, then my stomach felt upset, then my throat began to close. I knew I needed to see a doctor. My husband went out to get a cab, he took our daughter to a family member who was staying in the same hotel, and then he came to get me from our hotel room. But there was another problem: I was having trouble walking, and I felt very dizzy. I didn't understand what was happening to my body; cognitively, I was 100 percent there. When we got to the hospital, I realized I had lost total control of my left hip, which meant I couldn't hold myself up. My brain had lost the neuro-connections to the left part of my body, and I couldn't command it to move. We were in a different country; after four days, I had no clear diagnosis and was still waiting for test results.

A family friend knew of a doctor who lived in the city we were visiting. The doctor stopped by to see me. He spoke English and shared that he had worked for the Stanford hospital. He looked at my MRI and said I had vertigo and an inner ear imbalance. My husband and I decided to discharge me from the hospital. We felt confident because the family friend doctor assured us I would be okay. Then another setback: there were no flights going home that day. My vertigo was too strong. If I made a slight head movement the vertigo triggered a dizziness that would make me scream! And it happened . I patiently waited a day in the hotel room, avoiding movement as much as possible.

The next day we headed to the airport before dawn. My husband was pushing me in a wheelchair, dragging our luggage, and holding our two-year-old daughter. I felt tired and so afraid of falling sleep because I didn't want to experience an episode of vertigo in the plane. I will forever vividly and emotionally remember the moment the airplane landed in San

Francisco. Tears of gratitude rolled down my face, my inner being quietly yelled, "I made it home! I made it home!" The greatest moment of gratitude I've ever felt. The universe, God, and the Holy Spirit had kept me alive. There was a deep perception of hope, and safety. Throughout the process I had a deep sense of trust that everything was going to be okay.

I got to the John Muir Hospital's emergency department. The service was amazing. The first thing the neurologist believed I had was MS (multiple scoliosis) based on my symptoms: vertigo, loss of pain and temperature sensation on the right side of the body, loss of strength on the left side, loss of mobility of left hip, and double vision. But the test results came out negative for MS. **A CT Scan revealed I had a vertebral dissection (causing a stroke). Based on my great health and past occurrences, the neurologist concluded my stroke was caused by chiropractic manipulation.**

After a month in the hospital, I finally went home. I continued physical and occupational therapy for almost a year in which I re-learned to walk and my vision improved. I am not the same, but I accept my new normal. I can do a lot, and I am grateful for it all.

The reason I share this story is for you to dare and not wait for a traumatic life experience to happen before you step into your calling, your brilliance. You have the brilliance in you that is ready to shine now, towards what matters most to you. For me unfortunately, the stroke was the only way to force me to slow down. Yes, I realize I was stubborn and blind. I ignored the advice and promptings to slow down and enjoy the life around me. I thought I was enjoying life for the most part, but I was ignoring my dream, my calling. I had to be forced to slow down, but doing so helped me focus on what really matters most to me and created a determination to share my gifts and brilliance in the world.

My intention in sharing my story of how I was slowly able to bring forward the leadership and mindset work that energizes me is for you to see your value. My stroke and healing journey reminded me of how precious our time is and the importance of spending time doing the things that matter most to each of us. You and I have the brilliance to guide others who are stuck, held back, or blinded like I was. It is time to shine and bring forward your valuable potential to create and contribute. We are the community others need, a like-minded tribe who will cheer you on! If you know you are made for more, and you are ready to take on the challenge to move forward on what's calling you . I believe there is a reason why you're reading this story.

I started my journey by learning to set daily intentions for personal and business growth. And learning to overcome the collection of old limiting beliefs and finding communities of support (includes a coach).

The beliefs and identities I had to change were many: The way I talked to myself, the way I related to myself, and the way I listened to myself. These identities were formed from my childhood experiences of feeling shame, loneliness, inferiority, powerlessness, and worthlessness. Even though I also experienced love, fun, and engaging family events, the traumatic experiences overruled and the feelings kept reappearing as a teen and adult.

I learned to develop a "New Relationship with Myself" (a mindset shift) in order to align with who I truly am. I will provide an example, but first I wonder if you have any limiting beliefs. Are there any factors limiting your growth and success? What are they? Please take a moment to journal what comes up for you. What are your patterns? If you need help understanding, look at the following list.

<u>Transform into a New Relationship with yourself. You can transform the old stories and bring who you are being into alignment with your true self and step into your brilliance by following the steps listed below:</u>

1. **Set an intention,** what do you want to create, contribute, or experience?
2. **What is holding you back? What are the limiting beliefs?**
3. **Who/What have you been blaming** as the reason that you can't succeed, create, or manifest? (Example: I don't have time/I am too busy, or they don't see my talent at work, I never get help from...)
4. **What is showing up externally? Any patterns?** (Example: Not taking action, fake productivity, always putting others first, clutter building up, I get disorganized, I am always late).
5. **What do you think others believe? What do you believe?** (Example: I am not being seen, nobody will show up to my event, clients will not buy).
6. **What are the deep feelings you are experiencing**? What was your answer to number 5 listed above? Use the following statement as "I am

. . . (Example: I believed I was not being seen or given the opportunity for a promotion: my belief was "I am not good enough," or "I am not prepared, not wanted, alone, not enough, worthless, too much, bad").

7. **Shift into the Brilliant you who is capable, wise, powerful, and resourceful.** Shift your focus and step into the part of you that really shows up for other people. Your strengths, talents, and the superpower you use to support other people in your life, to be of service to your clients or colleagues or where you bring your wisdom and contribution for others. **This is exactly what you can bring to yourself!** This is where your focus needs to be in order to uplift yourself and keep moving forward.
8. **Turn this care, attention, wisdom towards yourself and from this place of deep, positive connection with yourself, ask powerful questions.** Through breathing exercises and simultaneously quieting the mind you will find the answers you are researching for. For example, I wonder what my next step is? Who do I need to contact? How I am showing up? How might I find my power in these life circumstances?
9. **From here, focus on what is your next step?**

Here is an example of something I struggled with, which was feeling insecure.

- My statement was, "I am not good enough."
- The patterns showed up internally every time I wanted to create and bring forward important work. The patterns that showed up were experiences of deep insecurities, a lack of confidence, the absence of faith in myself, and a sense of fear. I tended to be perfectionistic and held unrealistic standards of performance and over-criticized myself.
- The pattern that showed up externally was procrastination. I avoided doing the work because I assumed it must be perfect in order to be accepted and I feared it would not be up to par. I overwhelmed myself by thinking and not doing. Or at times I would scan the room and compare myself to the most dynamic and powerful person in the room, making myself feel inferior.

The Shift to Brilliance:

The skills and capacities I learned to practice and cultivate to evolve beyond my false identity:

- Learning to shift my mindset and focus on my own strengths and talents, fully seeing and owning my own uniqueness and brilliance.
- Learning to name and reveal imperfections of beauty and brilliance in myself and each person I meet.
- Learning to appreciate the many shapes, sizes, colors, and forms that gifts and talents come in.

The next step to get momentum was finding guidance. I needed support to grow, to learn business strategies and more. I realized there was a lot I didn't know. I learned to start asking for help and being okay with asking (my excuse used to be, "I don't like bothering people"). I learned I could not do it all myself. I needed a team, a mentor, and a coach.

How to find your community of support.

For me it was trial and error. I started with a coach who helped me to act and write a plan. It took me a while to gain clarity of my new journey. I kept searching and found a community of small business advisors, a community of small business networks (there are many), a community of empowering women, a mom's community, mastermind groups, and more. How will you know which is the right community for you?

- Invest the time to get to know the community group.
- Learn their intention, values, and integrity. Ask questions.
- Ask yourself, "What support am I looking for? How will this community support my growth, my brilliance, my purpose? How do I want a community to make me feel?"
- Can you afford the community group membership now (some networks have a membership fee)?
- If you are not sure about the community support group/network. Take your time visiting the community before you commit to a membership. It's okay to say you're looking. Finding your tribe is golden.
- Look for a mentor and a coach. They each provide different support.

Here are the three things that helped me move forward with the work I care about.

1. **Set daily intentions.** Set time aside to accomplish one to three things that will move you towards your next step towards your brilliance.
2. **Discover your deeper truth**, stay connected to your higher self, and remind yourself of this new relationship with yourself when limiting thoughts pop up (see steps above).
3. **Find your community of support**, and always ask questions.
   Step Into Your Brilliance and SHINE!

Sonia Ferrell

Sonia Jimenez Ferrell is an engineer, leadership facilitator and coach, wife and mother. Through her initiatives, she has become a role model for women and an advocate of personal growth, compassionate communication, higher education, and adolescent education supporter through programs such as STEM, Puente, MESA, and Girl Power. Sonia has been mentoring and coaching college students for the past 18 years, while working as an engineer. She received a B.S. in Industrial Engineering, a master's degree in Leadership, and a Values Coach accreditation.

After recovering from a stroke when her daughter was two years old, Sonia decided her calling was working with people. She has shifted her direction towards helping individuals and businesses succeed and align with purpose and values in order synthesize powerfully and effectively.

She specializes in delivering trainings, workshops, and values coaching for individuals and new managers. Sonia leverages Emotional & Social Intelligence to help individuals and emerging leaders tap into their roles and potential by developing self-awareness, resilience, focus, and management skills. She coaches and helps individuals understand their foundational values, the values they want to bring forward, and guides individuals to develop the skills desired to bring forward and live by.

Sonia is also a member of the Association of Talent Development. With a focus on positive change and empowering impact, Sonia continues to collaborate with the Leadership Center at Saint Mary's College bringing the leadership work to helping communities.

Sjferrell5@gmail.com
(925) 381-1360
FB: Sonia Ferrell, Training Specialist
LinkedIn: Sonia Jimenez Ferrell

EVERY TEEN IS BRILLIANT (AND SO ARE YOU)!

BY KIMBERLY SCHEHRER, MA

Have you ever heard someone say, “Teens have bright futures ahead of them”? Unfortunately, many teens don’t share this perspective; they act as if their future is pretty dismal, especially when they’re struggling in school. For over a decade, teens have walked into my office stating, “I hate school,” “I’m not a good student,” and “I’m stupid.” Their self-esteem has plummeted and their grades seem like proof that they’re right. **What teens don’t realize is that grades are just one sign of where they are today and shouldn’t be mistaken for where they can be tomorrow.**

I’ve seen it time and again, when given the needed tools and support, a teen can turn any situation around. Any situation. Why? Because *every teen is brilliant*. Even when they don’t hold that belief for themselves, I hold it for them. I know teens have a divine purpose and when they tap into their essence, they will soar.

Sadly, not enough teens have an adult—to whom they are willing and open to listen—standing for their brilliance. Without another perspective on how to interpret their challenges, their negative self-talk as a teen not only crushes their spirit throughout the school year but also stays with them into adulthood.

This is the reason I have so much love and passion for empowering teens to achieve their dreams through leadership skills. I am committed to having more teens see their brilliance, stop their negative self-talk, and break through what they had previously thought impossible. I stand for teens and invite others to stand for them, too.

What if we can support teens to step into leadership, feel empowered, and become unstoppable with their dreams and passions? I believe this makes all the difference in leading a fulfilling and joyous life. This is my heartfelt desire for all our youth.

Are any of our journeys easy?

I know the journey of moving through self-doubt, confusion, and victimhood because I was just like those teens sitting in my office, feeling stupid and not-enough. And I am not alone.

Many of us have felt despair, and we have also experienced triumphs. Yet, we tend to concentrate on our painful points, as opposed to feeling grateful for our lessons learned. My journey has definitely included injustice and pain, but I choose to focus on how the lessons I've learned can powerfully impact the parents and teens I serve.

As the youngest child in the family, I compared myself a lot to my brother, who is five years older. Now, looking back, he had five more years of growth and experience on me, so comparisons in my younger years would have always had me coming up short and/or lacking. While I struggled with learning how to ride a bike, my brother rode his with ease. When I told a knock-knock joke, my parents didn't laugh, so I believed I wasn't as funny as my brother (even though my friends laughed).

However, what cut the deepest into my feelings of inadequacy was that my brother was the first to be on the honor roll. See, I had difficulty in math *and* reading. I attended a summer program to help with my reading in third grade, which is all it took to get me back on track and "equal" to my peers. Unfortunately, I can't say I improved much with math; hence, no honor roll for me.

Since I was constantly comparing myself to my brother—and my brother seemed to be a lot better at everything—I imprinted the message "I am not good enough" into my subconscious and conscious mind.

Accordingly, I have empathy for teens who are struggling in school, comparing themselves to others, and feeling like they'll never be good enough. My message to them? Your struggles don't have anything to do with your intelligence, and certainly the implication that you are not enough or "stupid" is FALSE! I work with teens to explore comparisons in their life, tell their critical voice to stop, and refocus on gratitude for all the wonder-FULL in them!

If you are a parent, I'd also ask you to explore your role in keeping comparisons alive in your family, in your teen's peer circle, or even as a model of how comparisons affect your own life.

The Impact of Authority

Picture a quiet and shy child who is quite sensitive to others' comments. Teachers hold a lot of authority to a young child. One memory I hold crystal clear is my second grade teacher, "Ms. C," who used humiliation as punishment.

She made me wear a sign to ballet class that read, "I talk too much." Once she had me stand in front of the class, so all my peers could see the red birthmark on my left hand. My eyes threatened to overflow with tears as all my peers stood in a line to get a closer look. I couldn't understand why my teacher was turning her classroom into a freak show and having me be at the center of it. After all the unwanted attention, if Ms. C's intention was to have me talk less and hide out more, she certainly got her wish.

In spite of my childhood challenges with a few teachers, I do have great respect for teachers and have collaborated with many over the past decade to better the lives of teens. I know that most teachers are doing everything in their power to help their students succeed, which is why I tell the teens I coach that they can't judge all teachers based on a few bad experiences.

I also think we shouldn't underestimate the impact of what a child is going through as they're telling us about it. Teachers hold authority and thus, their messages carry a lot of weight for impressionable children. Anything a teacher says—especially that is negatively interpreted by a student—can affect a child's self-esteem for years to come. It is important for our children to see adults ("authority" figures) believing in them and supporting them, especially when they're having challenges with a teacher, another "authority" figure. I also believe that it is equally important to teach kids how to advocate for themselves because adults won't always be with them, and they need to be able to tactfully, confidently, and respectively stand up for themselves. It's a critical leadership skill.

Do you own your accomplishments?

In fifth grade, I finally got on the honor roll and maintained that status through middle school, yet I never understood how. To be honest, since I hadn't worked any harder than I had in first through fourth grade, when I received the honor roll award, I didn't own it or even think I deserved it. So, my self-esteem didn't improve much in my elementary and middle school years even though my grades did.

Is there an area in your life, past or present, where you haven't acknowledged yourself? Maybe it didn't seem like a "big deal" at that time, but retrospectively, it was significant. Please take a moment now and lovingly acknowledge your inner child, teen, or adult self for that brilliance. When we step into a place of self-acknowledgment, we step out of needing external acknowledgment over which we don't have any predictable control.

Slipping grades and steadfast dreams

By the time I was a junior in high school, my personal life was a bit chaotic. Since I didn't assert myself verbally very often, I bonded with the rebels and acted out instead of advocating for myself. My grades slipped,

I pushed boundaries, and my parents worried A LOT about my well-being. Yet, despite what was happening in high school, I was determined to realize two dreams after graduation: one was to be a parent and the other was to be a psychologist.

Although my dream to be a parent wasn't questioned by my family, my career dream certainly was challenged. My dad didn't value psychology and wanted me to focus on a business degree. My dad's disapproval of my dream hurt my heart because I valued his advice.

Dad always made a concentrated effort to treat my brother and me fairly, and he joked a lot about being "right." Being "right" was valued, so I never wanted to be "wrong." If I didn't speak up, then I would never appear to be incorrect or not-enough. He also got frustrated with me if I spoke out of turn.

Dad made a lot of my decisions. Theoretically, I "had a choice," but if my choice differed from what Dad thought was best for me, he scowled, a clear indication of disapproval. When I told Dad about dreaming of being a psychologist, the look on his face said it all.

In college, I did hold onto my dreams. Once I got accepted into college, psychology was the degree I pursued in spite of my father wanting me to pursue a business degree. This was one time I listened to what I call "my heart voice." Since I desired to have a private practice, which meant I needed a graduate degree, I knew I had to get better grades than I did in high school. With my vision in mind, I put forth my best effort in college. Yes, I had to take algebra and pre-calculus—my least favorite subjects in the whole world! However, steadfast in my dream of becoming a psychologist, I was in the math instructor's office every day to receive assistance and passed Intermediate Algebra with a B+ and Pre-calculus with a C!

Although getting a C might not seem like an accomplishment compared to other students getting As—retrospectively, it was a HUGE accomplishment to pass a class I never thought I would have been able to understand.

In all the other general education and specialty classes in the field of psychology, I received almost all As. I graduated college with Great Distinction overall and Honors in Psychology. I was ecstatic!

At the time, it was unheard of getting accepted into a PhD program with a BA degree. You had to have a master's degree or pursue your master's degree in the PhD program before continuing as a doctoral candidate. However, I was accepted into the Clinical Psychology PhD program at Pacific Graduate School of Psychology without having to receive my master's degree first. This was another HUGE accomplishment, and two Stanford University professors supported me with my dissertation, which was an honor.

After three years in the PhD program, I realized it would take me longer than four years to complete the doctoral program, and I was eager to start a family. Therefore, I decided to opt for an MA because of my deep desire for children, and my end goal of a private practice could still be achieved with a master's degree. I attended Santa Clara University for one year to complete my graduate degree and received my MA in Counseling Psychology with honors. My daughter was born early, so she was 6 days old—and with me—when I received my degree. My two biggest dreams were finally in my hands!

When we give our voice to someone else...

I gave my voice to my father in many ways, always asking for his opinion or advice. Who have you given your voice to, and on the flip side, whose voice have you spoken over?

One of the main reasons many teens don't open up to their parents is because they don't wish to disappoint them. I am not blaming my father since he too brings his childhood history with him to the present day. I mention this because when we give our voice to someone else, even a well-meaning and loving parent, it may cost us our self-worth. We can get disconnected from our voice, our vision and purpose, and certainly, become shut down to our knowingness or intuition.

At least that was my experience. I stopped trusting my intuition, and I feared sharing my opinions with the world because they might be met with disapproval, just like it happened with my father. I felt very small in high school, and this disconnection from my voice followed me into adulthood and motherhood.

Eventually, I became a mom to two beautiful daughters, and when I thought about what having "a voice" meant, it was in the context of protecting and advocating for them. However, when it came to me, I still acquiesced more often than standing up for myself.

Stepping out of my comfort zone wasn't easy, but I knew I had a bigger "calling" and always admired others who speak up. One day, I experienced a powerful meditation, which transformed my life, and it came to me: "To succeed, you have to struggle." So, in the footsteps of my father, I played to my strengths of perseverance, resilience, and determination, to step out of the shadows and give voice to what needed to be said to teens about being their best selves.

Fast forward to today. I am committed to impacting teens and their parents by sharing my voice through both public speaking and writing. I am passionate about public speaking because, for so long, I didn't claim my voice, and consequently my message was never visible—I didn't feel heard. If I hadn't had this particular journey, I may not have such a passion for public speaking.

Furthermore, I am expressing my voice by writing a book on teens stepping more into confidence and leadership, and how parents can empower and support them to shine (*Empowering Teens to Lead a Life of Purpose: A Guide to Support Parents and Teens* will be released in January 2020). This is powerful for me, and I am certainly shining in my brilliance when I speak and while I write. I look forward to continuing to help more teens find their voice and the best ways to express it!

Are you willing to tap into your infinite wisdom?

As I asserted at the beginning of this chapter: Every teen is brilliant. That also means every adult is brilliant since we were all teens once, right? So, how do you step into your infinite brilliance in spite of your current challenges, as well as childhood messages that may still affect you?

Increase your self-awareness and connect to your "heart speak" or intuition so that you can find YOU, your purpose, passions, and gifts.

Please take a moment and settle in a comfortable place with no distractions. Take three deep breaths and place your hand on your heart. Ask yourself this question, "What message is on my heart to share in the world?"

Notice what pops for you and what and how you are feeling in your body. An answer may not pop right away, or at all, and that is okay. However, by asking the question, without the expectation of an answer, it allows space for the answer to come to you randomly and have an "Aha!" experience. By doing this exercise, you are practicing self-awareness, and with greater awareness, you will begin to connect to your intuition and trust your knowingness.

Now go out and be bold, be authentically you, and share your message because it will impact others and help them embrace their brilliance too.

Brilliant Breakthrough Tips:

1. Honor your journey.
2. Claim your accomplishments.
3. Own your voice.
4. Connect with your truth, the message on your heart.
5. Share your truth, message, and voice. You are Brilliant; be willing to SHINE!

Kimberly Schehrer, MA

Kimberly Schehrer is a Teen Breakthrough Expert and Founder of Academy for Independence. She specializes in leadership, education, and personal development. She works closely with teens, who she feels are a misunderstood group brimming with potential. Kimberly has an MA in Counseling Psychology, three years in a PhD program, and over fifteen years of experience working with parents and teens as a Teen Breakthrough Expert, counselor, and an education specialist at schools, private institutions, and within the community in Silicon Valley and beyond. She is passionate about our next generation of leaders.

Kimberly's desire is for our teens to harness their greatest super power, themselves, just as they are, and up-level to unleash their full potential. Her passion is further ignited by watching them soar in the world to create transformation within themselves and their community. She nurtures our teens to lead their own lives according to their values, so they stand in their voice and confidently achieve their dreams with an unstoppable mindset. She is honored to have been cited in major media. Kimberly is a podcast host of "Teens Today, Leaders Tomorrow," a #1 international best-selling author and keynote speaker.

Facebook: https://www.facebook.com/academyforindependence/
Parent Support Facebook group: https://www.facebook.com/groups/2285499885030448/
LinkedIn: https://www.linkedin.com/in/teen-breakthrough-expert/
Twitter: https://twitter.com/AFI_LifeCoaches
Instagram: https://www.instagram.com/kimberlyschehrer/

WAKE-UP CALL TO MY AGELESS REVOLUTION
BY HEDDA ADLER

Five years ago, I had a wake-up call and received the shock of my life, when the doctor told me that I had a possible life-threatening illness.

My immediate reaction was, "No way. It's a mistake."

It was a critical time in my life, and I was under enormous stress. I recognized that if I wanted to stay healthy, I needed to make radical changes.

I realized that I had to find new ways of thinking, moving, eating, doing, and being if I wanted to thrive. My shift in attitude was an important factor in changing my life!

My physician is amazed to observe my health improvement over the last 5 years.

I chose to rethink everything. I ended destructive relationships that no longer served me, and I chose a new way of living! I have discovered keys to living a vigorous, youthful life. I am actively disproving the myths about aging, that we lose our potency, our flexibility, sensuality, creativity, and ability to enjoy life and be a contribution.

I grew up in post-war Germany. My parents were full of dark tales of the war that colored my view of the future and gave me nightmares. I grew up fearful, despondent, and depressed. I remember every time when my younger sister and I were fighting, my mother always lashed out at me, hitting me in the face without asking for the reason. I remember her saying time after time, "Had I not given birth to you at home, I would have sworn that they had switched you in the hospital on me. You can't possibly be my daughter."

There was no way to defend myself against my mother. In order not to cry, I would tell myself that I am good. I am special. I am a princess. I would say this over and over again. This was my mantra at a young age. I used it as my lifeline. It was many years before I understood the meaning of the word.

There are parts of my life that read like a fairy tale and other parts that resembled a horror story. I sustained deep emotional pain. I did my best to be a good girl, get good grades, do what I was asked to do; nothing mattered. I had a deep, unfulfilled longing to be accepted, cared for, and acknowledged.

When I was twelve years old, the situation with my mother and sister led me to want to end my life. I devised a plan. There was a pharmacy in town. I went there and told the pharmacist that my mother needed medication; she was having bad headaches and nausea and couldn't leave the house. The pharmacist believed me. I was given the medication and the instructions to tell my mother.

The day I took the pills, I remember it so vividly. It took so much courage to end my life.

I was in so much emotional pain, felt unwanted, unloved, and punished for things I had not done. I hoped that those 60 pills would permanently take me away from my mother and sister.

It started to rain. I walked deep into the forest, familiar to me since it was our extended playground all year round, specifically in winter when we enjoyed our sleigh rides.

As the drugs took effect, I became disoriented and sleepy. I woke up drenched with rain, shivering, huddled next to a giant chestnut tree. I was so cold that all I wanted to do was die in my own warm bed. Staggering home in a daze, I stepped out of my wet clothes and threw them under the bed as I slipped under the covers.

In the morning, I was still in a deep sleep; I heard my mother repeatedly yelling in the distance for me to get up and finally pulling the covers off me. All I could think was, "Oh, my God, is she here in heaven, too?"

I struggled for weeks to recover, and I had only one wish: to leave my family as soon as possible. Seven years later, after I had finished school, the opportunity arrived when I got an invitation to interview for a secretary position in Hamburg.

On the train from Cologne to Hamburg, a very sophisticated middle-aged gentleman gazed through the restaurant coach for a seat to eat. The only available chair was at my bistro table. I was so shy at the time and hoped he wouldn't ask to join me. When he did, I couldn't say no. I said yes instead.

How little did I know that my "yes" would change my life forever; it was the beginning of a modern fairytale.

He was assigned to live for a year in Hamburg, and he invited me to join him for the following weeks to discover that beautiful city together.

I was just an ordinary girl from a mid-sized town in Germany. I fell in love with a man twice my age, very distinguished and charming. He was accredited in Germany as the military attaché at the Iranian Embassy of Cologne.

He was a member of the Iranian royal family. When we found out that I was pregnant, he informed his Majesty, and we had a Persian marriage ceremony in Paris.

Three months after my 20th birthday, September 1966, I gave birth to my real little Princess Colette in Cologne, Germany.

After his tenure ended, we left Germany and drove by car to Iran. The next four years were magical. We were swept into the life of the royal family. That special time ended with the revolution. My daughter and I were lucky enough to escape the country before Khomeini and the Mullahs changed the course of Iran completely. My daughter and I returned to Germany. Colette's father couldn't leave the country, and sadly he passed away.

Several years later, I accepted the invitation from a friend of the family, then living in California. Our daughters were friends and had shared fun times together in Teheran.

I arrived July 5th, 1986 in Clayton, California to explore the possibility of living and working in America.

Caught up in the dream of a new life, I overlooked the red flags that popped up here and there. I accepted the marriage proposal of my Iranian friend. I was excited about getting married at Yosemite National Park and being queen for a day. This moment in time of absolute emotional ecstasy made me unaware of first signs of shadows that became eventually dark emotional clouds challenging my strength for years to come.

That very first night, I realized that his friends were far more important to him than his new bride was! They were lost, and he was waiting for them to arrive. When they finally did, they had missed our ceremony, and he spent half the night with them into the early morning hours. I had fallen asleep in my room. There was no explanation, no waking me up, no kiss good night.

It turned out the wedding itself was the apex of our marriage, and the one sweet memory for a long time. My new life was full of emotional challenges. I took care of everyone living in the household, including my elderly mother-in-law who needed hospice care. During those 2 years, I refused to succumb to self-pity. Thank God, little did I know that I would allow myself to be held emotionally hostage for the next 28 years.

In 1994, my husband and I opened my Dermatiq Day Spa in Danville, California. Within a year, I had 5 aestheticians working with me. My hallmark became pre- and post-plastic-surgery assistance.

I had unique skills. I was the recipient of the highest international accreditation in the field of aesthetics, and I had "hands-on" multicultural experience in skin care. I knew I could contribute to improve women's skin and lives, and this gave me a sense of accomplishment.

My business took off and I quickly became known beyond the San Francisco Bay area for my unique and effective treatment methodologies. My thorough education and my personal passion to work and study in France, Italy, Switzerland, Germany, and Iran gave me the privilege to observe ancient beauty rituals of Middle Eastern women.

My approach to skin care and total wellness is a tapestry of woven experiences combined with education and modern-day technologies that has kept my clients excited, loyal, healthy, and ageless. This has remained true for the past 50 years.

During the Danville Spa years, internally, things were different. Everyone thought I was a happy, successful businesswoman married to a handsome man, adored and envied by many. Nobody knew that all my life I was insecure and battled lingering childhood wounds holding me in a tight grip. My relationship with my husband had eroded to the point that I ended up severely depressed and in dangerously poor health.

When I asked my doctor for an anti-depressant, he denied it. He wanted me to sit alone and dig deep into my soul to find the culprit and change the root cause of my health condition.

I knew then what got me there: years of emotional and physical emptiness. I no longer could afford to ignore that situation. I had to leave to save my life.

Our divorce was final on March 28, 2013.

I moved from a 5000-square-foot home on 66 acres into a rented single room with one bathroom. I was free of my previous duties and now had time to relax and enjoy this newfound freedom. I was learning to letting go. I sat in the garden and listened to birds. I hung out with myself. I had peace and time "to be." All my duties as a wife of 28 years turned into the bliss of self-discovery.

For the first time ever, I connected with my Magical Soul.

A new, unknown world of spirituality, growth, and possibilities opened up to me. I finally woke up to the realization that this newfound awareness not only helped me to discover my unique gifts but also strengthened my character against all odds.

I discovered the power of manifesting and the power of my thoughts. This awareness helped me to educate myself about the need to keep my body healthy and change my nutrition. I eliminated sugar, bread, refined carbohydrates, and sweet drinks. I increased my water intake and exercised more. I was rewarded with the return of the figure I had in my thirties.

Friends and clients wanted to know the secret to my amazing transformation and begged me to share it with them. This led me to write my book *Ageless: 5 Keys to a Miraculous Life at any Age.*

My own journey taught me the most magical experience of my lifetime:

Everything we desire is possible for us to achieve.

If anybody would have predicted that at the age of 73, I would look decades younger and feel like 35 again, I would have never taken that person seriously.

At 67, when we divorced, I felt old. It was scary and difficult to hear his threats that I would end up with nothing, that I would be lonely with no family around. He was wrong.

I became compassionate and strong and started to ignite a fire in people's hearts.

I wanted them to experience a blissful quality of life again by removing any roadblocks to their total health and well-being. We do can do this by changing habits and stepping onto a path of total health ecstasy.

According to scientists, we are designed to live 100 years and beyond. If we are willing to change our habits and leave our comfort zone, which takes a strong determination, anyone can return to a healthy life again. Believe me, I know.

Let's unite against the overwhelming cultural manipulation about health and aging.

Who dares to determine that at the age of 40, we are already old?!

At 60, we are on our way out and at 70, we are supposed to live in an "Old Folks" home. Unimportant? Really?

Do we need pills for a quality life to survive?

We need to educate ourselves and learn about unhealthy food that makes us sick. Otherwise, we will continue to lose our health in the early years between 40 and 50, and we will struggle with low energy levels, getting depressed and taking more and more medication, which contributes to premature aging and death.

My skincare business, The Art of Ageless Beauty, continues to thrive. Now, I am starting Hedda's Ageless Revolution, busting the myth of aging by sharing our accumulated, invaluable wisdom. We can be the bedrock of stability in an ever-changing ocean of life. I ask each of you "Mature Wisdom Carriers" to join in, setting a new paradigm for human capability. I envision a renaissance of unleashed willpower that invigorates this beautiful, magical planet.

We need to get ourselves healthy first by nurturing and strengthening the healing capabilities in our bodies that have kept us alive up to this moment. We need to relearn its inherent power, study the healing ability of plants, and eat the right foods to support and strengthen our immune systems to be our trusted health allies.

I envision your return to health with the beautiful body shape, vitality, and bliss you enjoyed in the prime of your precious life.

Imagine that possibility!
Do you doubt it?

I am the walking, living proof that we all can regain a quality of life well into our 70s, 80s, 90s, and 100s. All we have to do is change our beliefs and redirect our focus and desires to enjoy the quality of our lives again. I envision an "Ageless Revolution" sweeping through this country.

I invite you to join together and become your own pioneer of the "Ageless Movement" and start dancing with life once again.

Tips To Claim Your Brilliance:

1. Pay attention to what you are speaking and believing into existence.
2. Spend time reconnecting with the true you.

3. Explore your why, values, and core beliefs.
4. Be courageous to take action toward your purpose.
5. Reclaim your health and vitality.
6. Be on purpose and on mission.

AgelessRevolution.com

Hedda Adler

Hedda Adler is an international speaker, award-winning author, wellness mentor, and skin-care expert. She is expanding and deepening the idea of longevity and exposing the deficiencies of our current "aging beliefs."

She is a recipient of the CIDESCO* Diplomat Certification Award, the world's most prestigious International Certification Award in Aesthetics. Hedda mastered the arts of Skin Care, Health and Wellness in her home country of Germany, as well as in France, Italy, Austria, and Switzerland. She has attracted a large and loyal following throughout her 50 years of supporting tens of thousands of women worldwide not only to look and feel their best but also to turn back "the aging clock" mentally and physically. Hedda is a leader in the increasingly significant shift in beliefs and attitudes that she calls "The Ageless Living Revolution."

She is the founder of the Meetup group, "Courageous Women in Transition – from Victim to Victor" A Miraculous Life At Any Age. Hedda is currently residing in the San Francisco Bay area of California.

*Comité International d'Esthétique et de Cosmétologie

hedda99@gmail.com
925-980-4773

YOU ARE ALREADY BRILLIANT
BY REV. LAURA JACKSON LOO

Hello, Beautiful!

This book is entitled *Step into Your Brilliance*. **I would like to welcome you to the brilliance that you already are!** Do you realize how magnificent you are? It's within you. It always has been. The most wonderful part is you don't have to do anything to be brilliant, magnificent, perfect, and whole. ***You are already that.***

If you don't feel like this, it's okay. Here are some questions to help you go deeper into your amazingness that I know you are.

What would it feel like to know there were no limitations in your life and what you could achieve? What would it feel like to know you were born with gifts and your soul's purpose is simply to shine? **How would you feel if you knew you were already perfect and whole, unconditionally loved and fully supported by the Universe / Source / God?**

Congratulations, you have arrived! Because it's all true—and then some.

By answering some of the questions above, I hope they weren't new revelations. If they felt like it, you merely forgot. It's all possible and THEN some. Just breathe that in for a moment. Feel how awesome your life can be. Because when you choose it, the Universe will show up to help you choose it.

It begins with saying YES to YOU. It's time for you to recognize and celebrate your awesomeness ***just for being you.***

Allow yourself to shine just by BE-ing you

Being 'who you are' and sharing your gifts means you get to choose YOU. That includes putting yourself first. When you put yourself first, you are able to more fully honor YOU, which means you are then able more fully to honor others. Pause and see how that feels in your body.

If you're a woman, this may feel a little more challenging. You may have felt the burden of being the caretaker, nurturer, mother, partner, provider, organizer, head of the household. Women historically have been the caretakers, the nurturers, the providers at home. Only in recent history have women stepped forward and upward into more equality, into opportunities not previously available in the patriarchy, illustrated in many arenas. The rise of the Divine Feminine has begun. The tide is turning. And the balance is re-anchoring.

Your diversity is our unity

Whatever your gender, ethnicity, religion, orientation—you ARE a magnificent being. ***There is no one on the planet exactly like you.*** Imagine how bright the planet would be if we all allowed our inner brilliance to shine fully?

It all happened for a reason

Here's another mindbender for you. ***You haven't done anything wrong.*** You didn't make any wrong choices in your life. You are not your past. You are beautiful, and you were learning, everywhere along the way. If this is something you can relate to, or where you may be in this very moment, you are not alone. I SEE you and I walk with you. You are here to shine brighter than the most glowing galactic star. **The reason you experienced certain life events was to help you realize WHO YOU ARE at your core, which is a beautiful, magnificent being.**

Here is my experience of saying YES, and how I held to this knowing while watching almost every aspect of my life be stripped away. Now on the other side, I know it had to happen in order to birth a beautiful new life with the rapidly blossoming opportunities.

My personal story of radical change and stripping away of the old

My life changed radically in the fall of 2015. I chose to make some difficult changes in my life that were ultimately for my highest expression. What transpired was almost daily chaos in watching my slate being cleared in every facet of my life. Already knowing some of my purpose for being on the planet, I fell to my knees, asking Source why I was here. Little did I know how my life would transform in amazing ways.

To paint the picture, I ended an engagement. I did not renew the rental lease on my townhouse. I put most of what I owned into a storage unit, struggling through the longest move of my life, physically and financially. Thinking I had a several-year housesitting gig, it turned out to be thirty days. Twenty-eight days in—and two days from being homeless—I found a dear woman in my spiritual community who said that I could stay with her for a while. I ended up moving a total of over four times over the next fourteen months.

Since I had little experience with supportive, loving relationships, I had given up on finding a loving partner relationship, much less getting married. My past love relationships could be defined by "working," "laboring," and "supporting" physically, emotionally, financially—for starters.

I was a single mother, though my daughter also moved out at the time. I was working a full-time job, commuting through a bridge-tunnel daily, and running three personal businesses. I gave free talks two or three times a month and was also a musician of forty-plus years.

Where am I today? More than "on my feet" and in gratitude for everything in my life. Since 2015, I have now moved five times. I'm happy to share the last time was recent and permanent. I met a wonderful man who is now my husband. We married fourteen months after meeting, and we just moved into a beautiful home together.

For the first time in my life, I am fully supported and unconditionally loved. We both support and uplift each other, laughing and sharing every day. I have the ultimate freedom in any moment— to write, research, meditate, give talks, practice my flutes, cook. I never dreamed this would be possible. And that's a biggie since I actually teach people how to dream big!

Here is my point. YOU can have anything you desire. I NOW SHINE BECAUSE I CHOSE MYSELF. I put myself first. I made difficult decisions in the short-term that were for my highest expression long-term. And in doing so, I knew I could do what I've always dreamed of, what is mine to do in this lifetime—and live in joy, all at the same time!

By putting myself first, I allowed the Universe to fully support me. Just like the Universe wants to do for YOU. It was hard at first. I spent a lot of time reminding myself to believe, to have faith, that it was all for a purpose, a divine purpose.

Where you are on the spectrum

Here's an indicator. If life is hard, difficult, heavy, or irksome, then you may want to take a deeper look. Take heart and know you can choose to be in a higher, lighter, and more joyful place within the spectrum of being-ness.

The spectrum I'm referencing is often referred to as the emotional spectrum chart. Would you be willing to go deeper with me? Wonderful. Everything in life is vibration: vibration of the food you eat, vibration of the clothes you wear, vibration of those in your inner circle, vibration of the music you listen to, vibration of your home.

Love and joy is at the very top of this spectrum, and hate and anger are at the bottom. If you are not happy where you usually "hang out," you can raise it!

Here's a clue: The lighter you become, the more joy you will have. The more joy you have, the more you can manifest greater things in your life.

There are many Natural or Universal Laws. They exist regardless of religious affiliation or personal beliefs. They just are. How wonderful is that? Why, you ask? Because when you know they exist, you can put them to work for you in your life.

One of the most well-known Natural Laws is the Law of Attraction. The Law of Attraction teaches us that like attracts like. That means if you only see the difficulties and hardships, that is exactly what you will attract more of. For example, when you are in situations where people complain, they often want you to agree with them. Have you felt your energy being drained in situations like this in the past? Consciously choose to step out of this energy or simply limit the time you spend in it.

Instead, look beyond your situation. Ask yourself questions like, "What else could this mean?" or "What more could this mean?" Then release any attachment or any more thinking about it. Choose activities or a state of being that is joyful and loving as often as possible, no matter what is happening around you. There are always things you can be grateful for. When you recognize your beautiful creative nature and consciously choose joy, you will begin attracting more of the same.

Out with the old and in with the new!

Have you heard the phrase, "getting rid of the old makes room for the new?" After talking about vibration earlier, now you have a little more understanding of how this can happen.

1. **Consciously choose to release what no longer serves your highest expression.** It doesn't matter what it is, relationships, situations, habits. It can feel overwhelming, but once you set a clear intention, you are calling in supportive energies. Then, when you physically act on it, you are further supported by the Universe.
2. Once you have released what no longer serves you—just like when you give away old clothes or items to non-profit charities—**you create a vacuum**.
3. The Universe DOES NOT LIKE a vacuum. Now that's not exactly true—the Universe doesn't like or dislike anything. **What's actually happened is by releasing something, you have made room for something to replace it**—and in this case, something fantastically wonderful.
4. **Now is the time to fill yourself up with wonderful visions of joyful and prosperous cocreations.** Hold the energy of "Yes, I would like this or something better."
5. **Then let go!** Because here's the deal. You get to set powerful and clear intentions about what you want. The rest is up to the Universe. Remember, the Universe figures out the 'how' piece. That is not yours to do. Because guess what? What comes back to you can be bigger, better, different, or more extraordinary than you ever dreamed. How does THAT feel?!

You are fully supported by the Universe

What do you have to lose by putting yourself first? What would you dream if you allowed yourself? How big can you dream?

When you love and celebrate yourself fully and completely, you will experience aspects of your life shift and change. Whatever happened to you, whatever experiences you've had, however much support you have had or not had, imagine that the Universe has been WAITING for you to step forward. When you step into who you truly are, amazing things will begin happening in your life.

Many millennia ago, humanity chose something special. Humanity chose free will. Free will is amazing because we can choose whatever we want. In this case, that includes choosing amazing new experiences that support you and your gifts unfolding.

Here's another aspect of free will. Because we, humanity, have free will, the Universe cannot violate our free will. ***This is why prayer is so important.*** The same holds true for setting clear and powerful intentions. The Universe, your angels, spirit guides, loved ones on the other side, are ONLY able to step in and assist ***if you ask and give them permission***.

I am inviting you to ask wholeheartedly for whatever you desire in your life in this very moment. Ask for what it is you need to allow you to "Step into your Brilliance!" It is time for you. I urge you to ask the Universe with clarity, conviction, and courage.

Knowing you are fully supported in asking for whatever serves your highest expression, the next step is about listening. Here are some ways you can connect and listen so you can step more into your purpose and passion.

Ways to connect for deeper intuiting

Stepping fully into your purpose and passion involves setting clear intentions and it involves deep listening. Listening for 'deeper intuiting' requires activities and surroundings that support quiet contemplation. Here are ways that can allow you to listen more deeply and hear more clearly.

- **Nature.** Nature is a conduit. Many people talk about the connection they feel and the insights they receive by walking in nature.
- **Meditation.** There are a zillion books on how to meditate. Here's what I recommend. Find what works for you. The art of meditation is about being in a "receiving" space. It is quieting the mind and mental chatter in order to hear the small, still voice within the heart. There are many tools associated with meditation, and they are just that, tools. Some people enjoy flowers or incense—their meditation being elevated from associations with certain smells. Some focus on a burning candle flame. Some will have pictures of Spiritual Beings, Ascended Masters, Archangels, Angels, Loved Ones. Know you are not praying to them; they are a conduit for you to focus. Here's how you know you are receiving divine inspiration and insights. If what you are hearing is positive and loving, that is divine. If it is NOT loving, it does not come from Source.

- **Music.** What kind of uplifting music do you listen to? You have probably heard that music can soothe the soul. That is the kind of music you want to listen to!
- **Say YES.** It's time for you. It's time to say YES to you! Know you are perfect, whole, a divine cocreator, and a magnificent being.
- **Fun!** You have permission in this very moment to release what feels heavy in your life, and embrace more lightness of being! Amazing things can happen when you become lighter and more joyful. And yes, you can actually be cocreating when you are having fun.

These are ways you can be more in the flow, what I call the Divine Flow. It is time for you and your gifts. Now you have the awareness to embrace you AND your gifts this lifetime. Watch your life transform into more magnificence than you ever imagined!

Anchoring your dreams into place

Did you know that you can have as many as 50,000 to 70,000 thoughts a day? Yep, that's what research shows. And you've probably heard you should write down your goals, that those who do can be more successful. Here is the metaphysical translation of that. When you write down your goals/dreams/intentions, you are helping them take form, physically!

What else does it mean? Begin writing! No, you don't have to be an author. Envisioning heart-centered intentions is good. If you want to make them more powerful, the next step is putting them on paper. You are helping to make them crystal clear to the Universe, and in essence helping to anchor them into physical reality. Wouldn't you like the Universe's immediate support with anything and everything you want to bring in?!

Overview of sharings

Below are tenets I've shared in this chapter. Remember, anything you connect to an "I AM" statement carries great power. You can rewrite some of the statements below to help anchor them into every aspect of your beautiful being!

- You are perfect and whole, unconditionally loved and fully supported by the Universe.
- Recognize and celebrate your awesomeness ***just for being you.***
- The reason certain life events happened to you is to help you realize WHO YOU ARE at your core, your beautiful, authentic self.
- The Law of Attraction teaches that like attracts like. Choose to be elevated and joyful as often as possible, no matter what is happening around you.
- Getting rid of the old makes room for the new.
- By putting yourself first, you are allowing and inviting the Universe to fully support you and all you desire.
- You are so loved.

Conclusion

What are you feeling in this moment? Do you feel more uplifted and elevated? Do you now see the Universe has actually been waiting for you?

I so love you. And the Universe so loves you. So why are you holding out? The Universe is just waiting to bless all your dreams, intentions and aspirations. It can begin in this very moment.

It IS time for you. ***You are fully supported.*** If you're already leading a remarkable life, what other amazing things could show up in your life? What support could you receive from the Universe that would allow you to reach even more souls?

You are fully supported to step into YOUR brilliance. The Universe, the angelic kingdom, your loved ones, your guardian angels and spirit guides, and so many other beautiful beings support you. And I support you.

So what amazing things are YOU going to cocreate? Because I can't wait to see!

Rev. Laura Jackson Loo

Rev. Laura Jackson Loo is a New Paradigm Thought Leader and Transformational Presenter. She is a nationally-recognized speaker on THE New Paradigm, Ancient Prophecies, Earth Changes, Metaphysics and Conscious Evolution. She is a speaker, author, consultant, mentor and musician who has been featured in print, on radio, and on television, and is a regular speaker at Edgar Cayce's A.R.E. (Association for Research and Enlightenment) since 2008.

As a national speaker, Rev. Laura provides a holistic approach by bridging Edgar Cayce's readings and ancient prophecies with modern science and quantum physics. Called the "Connect-the-Dots Lady," she shares how ancient prophecies have foretold humanity's evolutionary leap, *happening in this very moment*. Rev. Laura paints a beautiful mosaic of THE New Paradigm by interweaving ancient prophecies and Edgar Cayce's readings with future visioning, the new world of quantum physics, and viewing it all through a metaphysical lens, i.e., looking at the deeper meaning. Learn how you can transcend the rapid and 'surface' global changes and step into a whole new world filled with endless possibilities. The ultimate question is not what is happening to you, but what are you ready to cocreate in THE New Paradigm!

"Rev. Jackson Loo's insightful, joyful and heart-centered approach seamlessly reconnects people to their hearts, to Source, and to infinite possibilities within THE New Paradigm." For more, visit www.LauraJacksonLoo.com.

www.laurajacksonloo.com
www.soul-action.com
www.quantumcommunicationsllc.com
soulactionwoman@gmail.com

SECTION 2:

Claim Your Brilliance

KILL YOUR SELF-DOUBT TO LIVE YOUR DREAMS
BY GRACIE MILLER

Most people know Beyoncé as the fearless megastar known for her killer vocals and sexy dance moves. But for many years, who you were actually singing along to was Sasha Fierce, Beyoncé's alter-ego (1). The truth is that Beyoncé is kind of shy, and she needed an alter-ego to help her become the superstar she is today. So, she developed an avatar of herself, the confident, booty-shaking diva version of Beyoncé known as Sasha Fierce.

Beyoncé wanted to stay home with her babies and drink tea. Sasha Fierce wanted to shine her megawatt light all over the universe in a glittery unitard. Beyoncé wanted to watch Netflix and snuggle with Jay-Z. Sasha Fierce wanted to twerk up and down the stage at the world's largest outdoor music festival while bringing awareness to the plight of girls around the world.

See how Beyoncé needed some help to share her gifts? We all do.

Most of my work as a career and life purpose coach involves helping people come to terms with who they really are and how to share their gifts authentically with the world in a way that supports them. This involves telling the truth, not just to yourself, but to others, which can open us up to judgment and others' opinions. Even admitting you really don't know what you want to do can be scary because we're all supposed to "have it together." What if you make a wrong choice? What if you choose one direction in life and then can't pursue the other things you're passionate about? That's a lot of pressure!

When you're ready to share more of your gifts with the world, both the fear of failure and the fear of judgment can be very intimidating. On top of that, most of us haven't figured out how to let go of the idea that we aren't good enough in general, and because of that, other people's opinions weigh heavily on us. Even when the people close to us approve of our ideas, we still shy away from doing them because *who are we* to think we can get what we want or pull off a big change?

We know this self-doubt by many names: Self-Sabotage, Negative Nancy, Indecision, Analysis Paralysis, Not Good Enough, etc. Your particular brand of self-doubt will have its own name.

Self-doubt isn't actually something to be concerned about. It's extremely normal. But it needs babysitting. Believing in your fears more than you believe in your dreams is the mental equivalent of leaving a five-year-old in the house alone all day. He will destroy the house.

Don't worry, you can rebuild. You begin to rebuild with the following thoughts:

What's the absolute best that could happen?

What has worked for me to make a big change or tackle a challenge in the past? Can I apply that now?

Who is on my team, my support?

What would succeeding look like?

How will I feel when I've reached my goal?

What would Sasha Fierce (or your own alter-ego) do?

The things you think of doing that get you excited and happy—that's you. The things you think in response to it that make you sad, scared, or indecisive—that's not you, that's your judgment. You owe those thoughts nothing. Well, perhaps a "thanks for trying to protect me, but no thanks!"

If you are being called to do something, change something, or feel something, it's for good reason. Maybe you'll never be "good enough" in your own mind to make a dream happen. And maybe no one around you will understand why you're doing what you want to do. Maybe you'll even fail at it once or twice. But I'm here to tell you that you could be a full-on *bad person* (which we both know you're not) and still do cool things. You can try something, fail miserably, and then tweak it a little and still succeed.

Maybe you're considering a small change but it feels big. If it's been pulling at you for the last several years, guess what? It won't stop. Feel the fear and do it anyway. Even if you think you're not good enough. So *what* if you're not good enough? Why *not* you, anyway? No one deserves success more than anyone else. Did Britney Spears "deserve" success? Why don't you?

Your version of Sasha Fierce lives inside of you. If you are able to dream her up, she exists—if only in your mind. THIS is the person who is going to tackle your biggest goals from now on so that you can finally share your gifts with the world. Your inner CEO, Ms. Moneybags, whatever you want to call her, she works *for you* now. **You have this person in your corner all the time. She is your secret weapon of confidence and charisma.**

My alter-ego is sometimes a real person—a secret mentor, if you will. She has no idea that I use her as my litmus test for fear. Remember the "What Would Jesus Do" craze? Well I ask myself, "What would Sofia do?" If Gracie isn't feeling particularly brave one day but kind of needs to put the word out about an upcoming workshop, I ask, "What would Sofia do?" The answer is almost always that Sofia would put on her big-girl panties and shine her light on the world because she knows her light is a gift. And so is yours.

So who is this Sofia? Well, I got an email once from her that described her life very well. She is teaching workshops all over the world, swimming with dolphins, and writing a book while taking breaks to make love (yes, that was in the email). I know, right? UGH. I was so close to hitting Unsubscribe. And then I went, "Wait. I'm just jealous!" I'm jealous because I want her life! And if I know what I want, I *can* take steps to get there. If I know what I want, I have the power. There's no one to blame but myself if I don't go after what I want. Of course, that's when the doubts start creeping in.

I knew for years before I became an entrepreneur that I wanted to work all over the world doing transformative work with international personal-growth junkies like myself. That's not news. But the *how* eluded me for some time. Then I started taking courses in online marketing, sales, web development, and other things that I had no knowledge of before. And I could finally see the how. But something kept me glued to my familiar life.

Why *wasn't* I swimming with dolphins in Hawaii? Why *wasn't* I writing a book on top of a mountain with the occasional sexy break? I'm not a lazy person, so what gives? Simple self-doubt. A lack of belief that it's possible for me at this stage in adulthood. An insidious lack of self-confidence will do more to trick you out of your best life than any other barrier. I'm not even talking about low self-esteem but rather your basic garden-variety belief that you are not the special one who gets to do things like work abroad.

Beliefs like:

"It's too hard."
"No one has heard of me."
"I'm not 25 anymore."
"I don't have the money."

Blah blah blah. I've heard every excuse from my clients and, hilariously, I've heard them all in my own head too. **WE ALL HAVE THEM. It's time for the excuses and doubts to die. Either that, or *we die* with regrets.**

How to Kill Your Self-Doubt to Create the Life of Your Dreams

1. Write down all the reasons why you "can't" be successful (however you define success).

2. For every reason why you can't be successful, write out 3 logical reasons why you *can* be successful, even if you don't completely believe them yet.
3. Visualize yourself succeeding with each of the logical reasons you wrote down. Take a few minutes to *see yourself winning*.
4. Write down *how it felt* to win, to get what you really want. Do any new doubts come up? Are you concerned that others will be jealous of you or leave you? Are you worried that you can't keep up that success?
5. Repeat Step 2 for the new doubts.
6. If you are struggling with this, ask yourself if your alter-ego can do it "for you" or do it differently.

This is a process that can be done regularly to admit what's really stopping you and then rewire your brain for success. **People don't learn that they are incapable of greatness overnight. It takes a little while to undo what you've believed about yourself all these years that isn't serving your highest good. Think of your mind like a fixer-upper.** It's had some not-so-pretty things happen to it over the years, but with a little vision, it'll be the cleanest house on the block. I used to believe there was no way I could design my own website, find clients online, or be hired to teach workshops, but I do all of those things now. It's a process: Create goal → assess doubts → rewire your brain/ get help from your alter-ego to attack doubts → achieve goal (celebrate!) → create even better goal → repeat.

This is simply an invitation to ask yourself where in your life you may not be stepping up to your brilliance. What could life look like if you acted on that little voice within that tells you to share your gifts? Who might be inspired *by* you? What might you learn? And how much pain could you avoid by simply going for it, instead of hemming and hawing for years on end?

It may sound silly, but having an alter-ego works—just ask Beyoncé. She no longer has to use her old alter ego Sasha Fierce (2). Sasha Fierce was a useful tool, but she became limiting as Beyoncé was eventually able to accept herself fully and integrate all aspects of herself, even on stage. "Fake it till you make it" *isn't faking it* when you know you have that other aspect of yourself inside of you. You ARE that confident alter-ego, you simply call her by another name. So strut your stuff, Sasha Fierce. People are waiting for your brilliance.

Sources/Citations:

1. Beyoncé explains how she uses an alter-ego to perform in a way that she herself didn't feel capable of doing:

   http://www.oprah.com/oprahshow/beyonces-alter-ego/all:

(The second half of this article is all about Beyoncé and her alter-ego Sasha Fierce)

"The woman sitting next to Oprah is Beyoncé—but the force you see strutting her stuff in the music videos is actually her alter-ego, Sasha Fierce. 'She doesn't do interviews,' Beyoncé says. 'She only performs.'"

"Beyoncé says she crafted her stage persona to help her overcome challenges and give the best performances she can. 'It's kind of like doing a movie. When you put on the wig and put on the clothes, you walk different,' she says. 'It's no different from anyone else. I feel like we all kind of have that thing that takes over.'"

2. (Beyoncé discusses how she was able to "kill" her alter ego Sasha Fierce and finally be herself all the time: https://www.washingtonpost.com/blogs/she-the-people/wp/2013/12/28/finally-free-of-sasha-fierce-beyonce-is-a-grown-woman/?noredirect=on&utm_term=.37f298c2193e)

Gracie Miller

Gracie Miller is a certified Career and Life Purpose Coach who helps you stop settling, get unstuck, and love your life. Using both concrete block-busting tools and intuitive coaching skills, her goal is to help realign you with your most authentic self and communicate who that is in ways that support you. Through a structured process of identifying and releasing limitations and exploring who you really are, we can then create the life you were born to live. Gracie's passion and purpose is not just to help you find a better job; she wants to help you experience the freedom that comes from loving your whole life.

Since 2012, Gracie has coached people in all stages of life, from young professionals to executives, those returning to work after a break, business owners, aspiring entrepreneurs, and people who simply need some guidance to make it through a transition.

Gracie's mission is to help you embody the life you were born to live—personally, professionally, or both—and ignite a spark in you that inspires others to pursue their path as well. Whether she's coaching or reading the Akashic Records, Gracie's goal is to contribute to the spiritual evolution of the planet by catalyzing others to step into their brilliance.

Claim your free consult here:
http://www.livelifepurpose.com/free-consult.html

Social Media Links:

Gracie@livelifepurpose.com
Phone Number: 612-568-2123
www.livelifepurpose.com
https://www.facebook.com/livelifepurpose
https://www.linkedin.com/in/gracie-miller

LIVE THE MONEY STORY YOU WANT TO TELL
BY MARLENE ELIZABETH

Teach me how to trust my heart, my mind, my intuition, my inner knowing, the senses of my body, the blessing of my spirit . . . so that I may enter into my sacred space and love beyond my fear and thus walk in balance with the passing of each glorious sun. —Lakota Prayer

When the due date for the birth of my baby girl arrived and passed, my uncle lovingly said, "she's just like her mama, marching to the beat of her own drum." It's true. I've always been a creative, passionate entrepreneur at heart. And entrepreneurs are leaders. Servant leaders. However, it took me a long time to understand this about myself. As a result, I struggled during the first half of my life trying to find my place in "9-5" careers.

After college with a B.A. in International Relations from U.C. Davis, I began in a congressional office working on Capitol Hill with then U.S. Congressman Leon Panetta and later with U.S. Congressman Jay Kim, then went on to fundraising for the National Multiple Sclerosis Society. I earned my M.Ed. in Religious Education at Boston College and led spiritual retreats while also working as co-host of the national TV program *Word in the World*. The show aired on the Trinity Broadcast Network (TBN) and the Armed Services Network in over 100 million homes around the world.

Despite two college degrees and everything going for me, I felt a deep sense that I was missing my calling and not fulfilling my true potential as I struggled through financial hardship. There were times when those closest to me couldn't understand my perspective or decisions. I felt alone in a crowd and experienced more than a few dark nights of self-doubt, confusion, frustration, and fear. By nature, I'm a very positive person with deep faith. I couldn't understand my painful struggles around money and wrestled with this great divide between practical matters and following my heart to make a difference.

In order to live a financial story that brings us joy, meaning, and fulfillment, we need to step into our brilliance! What I mean by "brilliance" is living your authentic calling and purpose in your one precious life.

I grew up around a great dad who had spent most, if not his entire, career excelling in the world of retail management. I noticed during each visit to his stores that he was consistently well-liked by both the employees for whom he was responsible and the upper-management who signed his paychecks. In my eyes, my dad was a leader I greatly admired. So even at a young age, a part of me often wondered why he didn't just run his own company. I mean, how hard could it be if he already knew all the ropes inside-out from managing medium and large retail chain stores? The answer, of course, is "very hard," unless you're living your calling and purpose! Otherwise, it's just plain misery.

And that's why it's so very important to step into our brilliance so we can live the money story we want to tell!

So how *can* we actually step into our brilliance and live a money story we *want* to tell?

Despite our unique design for financial success, women still commonly struggle with under- earning. Women earn less than men in today's marketplace, and yes, experts point to countless "barriers" to explain this income gap, but some of this under-earning is self-induced, which is within our control to shift. Under-earners have several characteristics in common: *Under-earners undervalue their skills, talents and contributions; under-earners self-sabotage; under-earners fly under the radar.*

If you recognize any of these characteristics in yourself, I want to offer you some Brave Heart Tips:

1. **If you *undervalue your skills, talents and contributions***, start standing in your power and owning your worth and talents. It takes practice, but the journey leads you closer to achieving your financial potential. Recognize the value you bring to the world and be open to receiving the income you deserve for your skills, services, and/or products.
2. **If you *self-sabotage, know you're not alone.*** Most of us are guilty of self-sabotage at one time or another. Some of the common ways that self-sabotage shows up include procrastination, giving up in the eleventh hour of our miracle, spending too much time "dreaming" and not enough "doing," neglecting our self-care, being unforgiving when mistakes are made, not showing up, allowing negative people to zap our energy, enthusiasm, and confidence. It's important to understand how we sabotage our success, and we also need to understand why we're doing it. Listen to your self-talk; recognize self-sabotaging thoughts or habits. Then notice and honor what you need to do to get back on track, and gently focus back on what you set out to accomplish.
3. ***If you tend to fly under the radar, remember that success lies in stretching beyond your comfort zone. Taking risks regularly is important instead of routinely playing it safe.*** Risks can seem much bigger in our minds than they actually are. Believing in ourselves is a muscle we can practice by acknowledging and reassuring our fears instead of allowing them to dictate our choices. Practice courage stepping beyond your comfort zone, one brave feather at a time.

Above all, remember that change begins with choice. It begins with you. I encourage you to create a list of what is stopping you from allowing your financial success to unfold. Is it fear? Is it lack a support system for your journey? Could it be that you're relying on someone or some circumstance to save you, or maybe relying on someone to figure things out for you? Is it that your financial dream is not aligned with your values, strengths, skills, or passions? Or could it be that you've forgotten who you are along the way by putting everyone else's needs before your own? Or perhaps there is another reason that more closely describes your challenge? The important thing is to be honest with yourself and write it down.

Awareness creates a new way of seeing yourself and reveals opportunities once hidden from sight. It allows you to discover new solutions to old problems. Gently and bravely take ownership of your choices, remembering you are not alone! Together, when we take responsibility for our financial life—with compassion, forgiveness, and determination—we give ourselves the power to transform our financial circumstances and positively impact those around us. **Now is the time to embrace your unique value and gifts that you have been given, to experience the prosperity, peace, and joy that you deserve. Now is the time to love MORE and fear LESS as you step into your brilliance and unfold your feminine power to prosper.**

***

I'm crazy for quotes. Something I often do during speaking engagements is share quotes with a twist. Here's what I mean by "a twist." I find favorite, familiar lines and then add a financial lens to them. Suddenly, the quote transforms into a new and different way not only to see money differently but experience your relationship to it differently, too. Enjoy the mini-inspirational calendar below where you can adopt a theme each month in the year ahead to grow your moneywings™ based on one of the quotes below. Or add your own inspirational quote with a financial twist and mix and match! Then make a commitment and promise yourself that you will take a moment each day to check in with these daily quotes and think of one brave-feather action step you could take each day to help you stay aligned with each quote/theme each month. By the end of the year, you'll have grown stronger money wings! :)

01 | January: "Live the money story you want to tell."

02 | February: "Refuse to be financially ordinary."

03 | March: "Be your own kind of financial beautiful."

04 | April: "Believe in your financial wonderfulness"

05 | May: "Dare to dream financially."

06 | June: "Live the financial life you've imagined."

07 | July: "Don't dream your financial life. Live your financial dream."

08 | August: "Do something today that your financial future will thank you for."

09 | September: "Make today ridiculously, financially amazing!"

10 | October: "Enjoy the little financial things in life."

11 | November: "Financially speaking, **today** sounds so much better than someday."

12 | December: "Let today be the start of something financially new."

***

Today my relationship to money is grounded in *my own* personal values and truth as a creative, passionate, entrepreneurial Mom. The way I see it, money isn't about things. It's about people. Yes, money is important, not because of things we can buy, but because of the time and freedom it gives us to be with the people we love. **It isn't money that makes us rich; it's the rich experience money gives us to be with those we care about.** After all, we can always create more money, but time is finite. Keeping finances in balance like this helps me step into my brilliance each day as a parent, entrepreneur, and feminine leader.

I invite you to learn more about how money coaching can help you step into your brilliance and *live* the money story you *want* to tell by scheduling a complimentary chat with me at MeetWithMarlene.com. Thank you kindly for taking time to read my chapter inside this beautiful anthology!

Marlene Elizabeth

Like you, Certified Money Coach® Marlene Elizabeth has heard the phrase "financial security" defined in numerous ways over the years. Is it a magic number you reach? Is it a lifestyle you live? Is it power and influence? Is it being debt-free . . . finally? Is it meant for only a chosen few? Those with a knack for numbers, a college degree, born from wealthy parents, or just plain "lucky"? Or is there a different story? As a single, stay-at-home mom who's risen from financial hardship to becoming a highly-paid, successful "mamapreneur," Marlene's view is radically different. She shares with female audiences and clients that financial security is knowing **the safest place to be is believing in yourself.** Her #1 International Bestselling book MONEYWINGS™ (available on Amazon and Barnes & Noble bookstores) is a spirit-filled love-note full of inspiration for women to embrace their call to financially thrive.

Deeply motivated to be a financial role-model for her daughter, Marlene coined the term *moneywings*™ when her child was two to describe the unique capability women have to manage their attitude and mindset around money regardless of their financial story. Marlene believes that when you realize your **freedom to financially soar,** you can't help but unfold your own beautiful *moneywings*™ one brave feather at a time. Her sequel, "$top Doubting. $tart Daring: Weekly Wisdom To Live Your Dreams is due for release in 2020. Her deeply caring, strategic, spiritual, and innovative approach creates a safe harbor for women to connect, learn, and grow. Through her speaking, books and private one-to-one coaching, Marlene tenderly empowers women to answer the call to transform their relationship to money.

Get started today with a FREE MONEY TYPE QUIZ at
www.UnfoldMoneyWings.com
Email: Marlene@MarleneElizabeth.com
Phone: 909.562.2159
Website: www.MarleneElizabeth.com
FB: www.facebook.com/growmoneywings
LinkedIn: www.linkedin.com/in/moneywings

BABY STEPS AND FALSE BELIEFS
BY DR. RUTH ANDERSON

Stepping into my brilliance? I am not sure that means what everyone assumes it does. I find there are false beliefs that trip up many well-intentioned, large-hearted individuals and keep them from fully standing in their strength. I have shared the following beliefs and misperceptions about self-actualization in the hopes of releasing folks from self-limiting beliefs.

Faulty Belief: I have to do something large.

Stepping into one's brilliance does not always mean that our presence in the world has to be a big splash. **There are plenty of people who simply acted on what they felt in their hearts. That is all that they were asked to do.** Some, as a result, made a big splash without necessarily trying to. Take Rosa Parks for example. I am not sure that Ms. Parks woke up in Montgomery, Alabama on December 1, 1955 and thought, "I am going to change the world today." I would guess that afternoon when she was ordered to relinquish her seat on the bus, she simply thought, "I have had enough." She spoke from the heart, refused to stand, and as a result, she changed history. Rosa Parks stepped into her brilliance without even trying to or knowing it happened at the time.

Stepping into your brilliance can be done on a daily basis, one small step at a time. Some days, my brilliance shines most when I am simply being the best me I can be on behalf of someone else. As a mother of two teens, I get that opportunity frequently to put their needs and desires before my own. Recently, on a vacation to Galveston, Texas, we took a day to shop for prom dresses in Houston. Was that my first choice of how to spend the day? Maybe not. Did it bring great joy to my daughter? Absolutely. Did I model for my daughter something I call "palpable love," a love so obvious that you can see it, hear it, and touch it? You bet! Her appreciation for our spending an entire day of vacation devoted to her finding the perfect dress made sacrificing the day at the beach totally worthwhile. For that day I was brilliant as her mother!

We are each capable of brilliance.

Stepping into your brilliance means bringing your best self into the world. Maybe you don't believe you have the capability of being brilliant? Oh, but you do!

Each and every one of us is capable of brilliance. Whatever story you have playing in your mind that makes you question your worth or ability to bring anything of value to the table, consider that it is simply your perception and not based on reality. Feel free to question what you believe to be true about yourself. Remember that the universe needed one of you to make the world a better place. And here you are! I know that you are worthy of brilliance!

"Most of us do have a smaller vision of who we are, and in the world of spirit, they are very anxious for us to know how much bigger we are and to step into that."

-Sumaya O'Grady, Soul Alchemist

Faulty Belief: I need to be doing something in order to be worthy.

So, does stepping into my brilliance demand that I am always doing something? Isn't it enough sometimes just to be? In order to be brilliant, do I need to become something? What about people who aren't able to do much because of health constraints? I venture that their ability to love, share compassion and listen to others is, in itself, a form of brilliance. What a gift really to be loved and listened to by someone. Are this person's contributions any less brilliant and needed on our planet?

One day recently I provided a reading for a mother of a young boy with very high energy and special needs. She was so busy caring for him that she felt incapable of being a lightworker assisting others. In meditation, I thought of this mother and her frustration. I was given a vision of a lighthouse. I was reminded that a lighthouse simply stands there and shines so boat captains can navigate to safety. Lighthouses don't go out looking for boats to save. As a lightworker, this mother could stand in her energy and God's divine white light. Others could see and feel her presence and be impacted by that. When her son was more grounded and stable, she would have the opportunity to get out into the world and continue her work.

Share your gifts with others.

My mother lives in an assisted care facility. The other morning as I sat in the front reception area, the body of a resident was wheeled out on a gurney by the coroner. Six members of the staff had escorted her to the door; each one of them was crying. This woman had been living in the memory care unit. While she had been a mere shell of who she had been in her earlier life, she was beloved by so many. This facility is a place where people go to die. Yet here she was in her final months of life, and she was touching hearts, sharing the brilliance of her true self, her true soul. Don't tell me that you have nothing to give others. You have yourself. And that self is enough that will bring others to tears at your passing, just for the fact that you are no longer with us.

Friends, if you can't bring anything else to the table, bring love. I believe that we are here for one reason; our one duty as a human being is to love others. Everything else is adding betterment to the planet. But everyone needs to feel loved.

Create a Body, Mind, and Spirit Connection

Over the years, I have learned to follow my own advice. I allowed myself the grace to stop achieving in the ways I thought others expected of me and took the risk of working with my body, mind, and spirit together with one combined intention. As a result, I have been able to step into my calling with grace and knowingness. I have been able to understand and expand on my gift of intuition. I have stepped into a future I could not have thought possible, working with archangels and the Divine Mother, and co-authored three books with Spirit. As the founder of Enlightened World and EWN, I created a platform for lightworkers to build their professional visibility through articles and podcasts in order to bring more divine light into the world. I suppose, I have stepped repeatedly into my brilliance, and have seen the compounded results of changed lives.

Faulty Belief: I must have my act completely together before I am worthy of helping others.

So many people, women in particular, use this excuse as a justification for staying small. If I am not 100% put together, how can I possibly teach a class, write a book, or host a podcast? I will be the first to tell you that no one, literally no one, has everything 100% put together. So, what percentage do you think you do have your life pulled together? Fifty-eight percent? Seventy-nine percent? The way I see it, if you are 79% pulled together, that means that 78% of the people could learn from something you have to share. So go ahead, teach that class, start writing that book. Someone can benefit from reading your life's experiences and hearing your point of view.

If I stand in my calling, then the people I care about will shun me.

I know from firsthand experience that there may be some truth to that. And that is ok. **We do not need to stay small so others feel more comfortable around us.** The fact that they would want us to stay small shows us that they are out of alignment with our own growth and potential trajectory. Have you ever outgrown someone? It doesn't mean that you need to release them from your life forever. It might just mean that there may be others whom you have not met yet who are able to support you better on your path.

I was very hesitant to share my spiritual transformation with my father. I thought he would be judgmental or closed-minded. I finished writing my first book *One Love: Divine Healing at Open Clinic* when my father turned 86. He was diagnosed with mesothelioma, cancer of the lining of the lung. As his time on Earth was limited, I knew that my time to "come out of the closet" was limited. I gathered my courage and gave him my completed paperback. He read it cover to cover. Over lunch, my father shared his concern that people might judge me harshly for writing about being intuitive. He shared his life experiences about hearing Spirit and having a connection to spiritual guides who impacted and guided his career for the last 30+ years. My father, from whom I feared the most judgment, turned into one of my greatest allies! All I had to do was gather the guts to share my truth and stand in my own energy. A year later, as I sat with my father at his deathbed, he and I walked through his passing together. This was an immense gift for both of us, that could not have happened without the closeness we had shared his final year of life.

Faulty Belief: It is best not to stand out.

Like the facets on a diamond, we are all unique, yet integral to the whole. We are unique for a reason. If we were all exactly the same, then there would be no diversity and no richness coming together to make life more interesting. I find that the individuals who really stand out in life are the ones who have embraced what makes them unique, steeped in it, and made it their signature style.

Sometimes, in my work as a lightworker, I feel like I am out in left field all by myself. But that's okay! I am following my calling. And it is okay for you to follow your own calling as well. Not only okay but imperative! **The world needs each of us to be conscious about fulfilling our purpose, even though our callings don't look like anyone else's. And because our callings don't look like anyone else's, it is even more imperative that we all participate!** By following your calling, doing what you came here to do, it shows others that it is okay for them to be all that they are meant to become. So please, be brave, stand in your light, and follow your calling. We are counting on you! My friends, Hugs to you on your journey! May you find love and grace along the way.

Steps to Step Into Your Brilliance:

1. **Be Patient.** If you don't know what your calling is just yet, be patient and eventually it will be revealed to you.
2. **Find your tribe.** Surround yourself with people who are like-minded to your beliefs and will support your fully stepping into your power.
3. **Be brave.** Dig in, dig deep, and be braver than you ever thought you could be.
4. **Share your gifts with others.**
5. **Always bring your best self.**

Dr. Ruth Anderson

Dr. Ruth Anderson is an award-winning, international best-selling author and founder of Enlightened World. Retired after a satisfying and worthwhile career in special education and public-school administration, Ruth embraced her second calling, that of an intuitive reader and healer. After becoming a Reverend of the Church of Inner Light, she was given a ministry to witness and participate in the healing of souls with and without bodies in the ethereal realm called Open Clinic. Ruth serves as a conduit for the Spiritual Divinity and shares their teachings in an authentic way and open manner.

Author of *One Love: Divine Healing at Open Clinic*; *Walking with Spirit: Divine Illuminations on Life, Death and Beyond*; and *Listening to Light: Love Letters from Walking with Spirit*, Ruth is passionate about sharing her experiences with the Spiritual Divinity and Divine Healing Beings. Believing that lightworkers are often isolated and distracted from sharing their gifts, Ruth was led to create Enlightened World. Enlightened World Online and Enlightened World Network serve to support lightworkers in building their professional visibility so they can get back to sharing their lightworking talents with the world at a time when it is desperately needed.

www.enlightenedworld.online
https://www.facebook.com/theministryonline1/
https://www.theministryonline.org

RECLAIM YOUR BRILLIANCE
BY DR. MICHELLE PETICOLAS

We all come into this world with *brilliance*. It is the spark of life. It is our personal connection to source, the universe and all that is. Our mission in life is to translate that spark into material form through our unique gifts and genius.

You can see that spark, that brilliance in the eyes of a newborn child—a shining wonderment that is alive with possibility.

Unfortunately, our brilliance often becomes overshadowed by the physical demands of human existence and our body's drive for survival.

My own wide-eyed wonderment, apparent in my earliest photographs, had already shifted into a knitted brow of concern by the time I was two.

It was not an extraordinary shift but rather a common one. Navigating this human world is complex enough to give any young person a frown.

We begin life at a huge disadvantage, with barely functioning bodies and limited communication skills, e.g. laughing and crying. We are forced to rely on our parents and caregivers for our most basic needs. Very few of them understand what is truly required for us to thrive. By focusing on survival, we can lose connection with our brilliance.

I was the 3rd child of a young mother. She was already overwhelmed by the needs of my two older siblings, so we never bonded. I suspect she had bonding issues of her own, an unfortunate pattern carried through generations.

I did bond with my father—briefly. He was a Major in the U.S Army during World War II and was transferred to Japan during the occupation when I was barely two. This untimely separation left a lasting emotional scar that has reverberated throughout my life.

To survive, I developed the habit of pleasing. It is a habit that is encouraged in women, even today. Being a pleaser worked very well for me at home and in school. It gave me attention and approval: National Honor Society, Phi Beta Kappa, and finally my Ph.D.

The problem with pleasing, I have discovered, is that it can hold you back from fully sharing your brilliance.

My people-pleasing success in school did not transfer well to the work-world. At my very first adult job as a sociology instructor at a small midwestern college, I tried everything—I joined the faculty committees, taught new classes, night classes, adult education classes and even coached the women's cross-country team. Yet, I lost that job.

I was devastated. My plan for obtaining love and approval had failed me. I became depressed, sick, and floundered my way through the rest of the term. Then, I ran away.

Instead of abandoning my pattern of pleasing, I modified it. Thereafter, I only took jobs where my bosses needed me more than I needed them. I undersold my education, my skills and my brilliance.

Throughout this period, I continued to work on my Ph.D., which I completed a few years later. I expected the world to open its doors with this achievement. IT DID NOT!

When I asked my father what he thought about my doctorate, he told me that it made him feel ashamed of his own lack of academic success. He never earned his college degree. Oh, great! My achievement caused my father pain!

Then I asked my boss to introduce me to our clients using my new Dr. title. He laughed and suggested I have it tattooed on my forehead. Humiliated, I did not refer to that title again for many years.

The same boss who humiliated me about my Dr. Title also promoted me. Then he fired my husband. Not an ideal setup for marital harmony. Soon after, my husband left me.

It seemed the world was telling me: "Stay small! Don't excel. Forget your brilliance or you will be rejected and abandoned!"

So, I joined a spiritual community where careers and relationships didn't matter. The only thing that mattered was connection to the divine.

Some guardian angel must have been looking out for me because this spiritual community actually opened up my heart and reconnected me to my brilliance. I received daily lessons in letting go of my fears, quieting my thoughts and connecting with spirit. By the time my current husband arrived on the scene, 13 years later, ***I was ready for love.***

WELL, not quite!

When we left the exalted atmosphere of the spiritual community, it quickly became apparent that I had major emotional issues. My fears of rejection and abandonment were sabotaging our budding relationship. So, I went to California and enrolled in a therapeutic program to heal my early childhood wounds.

Shortly after completing this program, my parents began to transition. First, my father died from Alzheimer's. Then my mother's breast cancer returned.

I went back home to New Jersey to help her finish up her business. My mom was a toy designer. In partnership with my aunt, she sold toy concepts to major New York companies including Gund, Hasbro, EG Dolls and Sears. Although, they never made it big—i.e., they never achieved that million-dollar benchmark—they had a great time and even had a significant impact on the toy industry.

I was not impressed with my mother's achievements when I was a child. It reminded me of my insignificance in her life. But in that final visit with her, something huge shifted inside me.

We were siting in her studio going through papers. I picked up a photocopy of one of her designs and asked, "Do you need this anymore?"

My mother looked at it and sighed, "I guess I'll never finish that project."

Her words pierced my heart. In that moment I understood what DEADline REALLY meant!

A complexity of feelings rushed through me. I was afraid. I took the paper back and said, "We don't need to do this right now."

Instead of holding space for her to explore her regret, to face her dying, I shut her down. That moment of intimacy, the intimacy I had craved from her all my life, was lost— forever.

She died two weeks later.

My mother's moment of regret became MY MOMENT OF REGRET!

It was her parting gift.

In that moment she transmitted to me the most important message of her life and mine:

LIVE WITHOUT REGRET!

The experience catalyzed me. I would NOT live with regret; henceforth, I would follow my passion!

A short time later, I began working on a documentary, a film about death. My mother's death had transformed me. I wanted to wake others up to its life-changing power. I wanted people to understand that awareness of death is essential to living without regret.

I joined hospice, interviewed people and learned essential secrets of living and dying. The film morphed into a 3-part series: *Secrets of Life and Death.*

Many times during the ten years it took me to complete the series, I worried about failure. Who did I think I was? I had never made a documentary. I didn't have the equipment. I didn't have the funding! I didn't even know what I was doing.

But the memory of my mom kept me going.

When the films were finished, I had to distribute them myself. I was learning as I went. I held screenings and workshops and figured out how to sell them to universities online. Eventually, I received three grants from The Lloyd Symington Foundation to bring them to the cancer community. There, I connected with people who were dealing with loss every day.

Building on these experiences and the work I did at hospice, I became a coach, helping people struggling with grief and loss. I saw loss as a doorway to transformation, like it was for me, and empowered them to reclaim their lives. My coaching has enabled me to pass along my mother's lesson: *live without regret.*

I have discovered three basic keys in making this happen. They are Brilliance, Body, and the Brain.

Brilliance, of course, is that spark of life, our connection to source, the universe, and the divine. Brilliance is who we *really* are.

Body is our physical container in this 3-dimensional universe. It is the mechanism by which we translate our purpose and special gifts into material form. We can't fulfill our life mission without body. But it has its own agenda—keeping us safe and alive—which can put it at odds with our Brilliance.

Brain is an amazing organ that enables us to learn from the past, problem-solve, and plan for the future. It assists body in keeping us safe through its beliefs and behavioral directives.

In my own story, a fear of rejection and my pattern of pleasing helped me feel safe but disconnected me from my brilliance. Through spiritual and emotional work and my mother's message, I have reconnected to my true purpose and my brilliance.

When brilliance, body, and the brain work together in harmony, it is possible to live fully and without regret.

Below are a few practices that can help create the balance:

1. Do things you love to do, e.g., walking, dancing, singing, drawing, playing with children, etc. Do them every day. This will boost your brilliance. If you don't know what to do, experiment. You will know what you love by how it feels in your heart.
2. Check inside and listen to your inner voice, the one that whispers with curiosity and courage. This voice will guide you in your mission. Whatever it says, write it down and then make it bigger. Imagine how you will feel when you achieve your dream. Think about it everyday. It will activate support from the universe.
3. Pay attention to synchronicities and affirmations. They are those little daily incidents that say "Yessss, you are on the right path!"
4. When feelings of fear, anger or sorrow arise, have compassion for yourself. There were good reasons why you hid your brilliance when you were young. Reconnecting to who you really are can trigger old fears. You can release the fear by focusing on the sensations in your body. This only works when you stop your brain from making up catastrophic stories. Negative thoughts will put your body into fear mode.
5. Master your thoughts. Notice what you think about. Is it uplifting or full of fear? Try limiting your consumption of media that feeds negative thought and increase your consumption of uplifting material. Changing negative thoughts is a matter of practice that gets easier with repetition.

There is one more key to living without regret: community.

Community is made up of family, friends, colleagues and culture.

Remember, we are social beings designed to bond. When we feel connected and loved, the body feels safe and secure. When we are rejected or criticized, the body will react as though threatened. Community, therefore, has a huge influence on how we think and behave. It can encourage us and make our way easier, or hold us back and keep us stuck.

My fear of rejection kept me playing small for years. I had to shift my thinking and overcome my fears in order to replace this pattern. Changing my community, i.e., joining that spiritual group, enabled me to start my transformation.

How about your community? How well are your social needs being met? Do an inventory. Are there any changes or adjustments that might make things better? Take action and see what happens.

We live in a time of tremendous change. The old system of fear and accommodation is no longer working. It is causing the decimation of our environment, infrastructure, and social institutions. My experience suggests that things may get worse before they get better. We rarely change unless we absolutely must. I believe we are being pushed through the doorway of change and it is time to respond.

By stepping into our brilliance and fulfilling our life purpose, we actually help not only our selves but also the world.

Isn't that an inspiring idea!

Be who you truly are and live—and die—without regret.

Keys to living and dying without regret:

1. Brilliance – Connect with who you really and truly are.
2. Body – Translates our purpose and gifts into material form.
3. Brain – Problem solves, plans, and brings our purpose forward.
4. Community - Supports you, loves you, and uplifts you.

Dr. Michelle Peticolas

Dr. Michelle Peticolas is a best-selling author and award-winning national speaker. She empowers leaders and change-makers to overcome their fears and limiting beliefs in order to step into their authentic power, make a difference and live and die without regret.

She has a Ph.D. in Sociology and Psychology and over 18 years of coaching people through major life challenges. Drawing from current studies in neuropsychology, evolutionary biology, and psychosomatics, and 35 years of spiritual practice, Dr. Peticolas has developed exercises and tools that promote body intelligence and mental mastery.

She leads workshops for universities, hospitals, and professional organizations throughout Northern California, including The Commonwealth Club of San Francisco, University of California Medical Center, and University of California Berkeley. She has presented to diverse audiences interested in enhancing and developing their awareness, skills and effectiveness in managing and coping with change. Her unique programs, "Release Your Grief and Thrive," "No Regret Now," and "Magnify Your Mission" are designed for professional women navigating the challenges of life. Her programs have received praise for their structure, design and powerful impact in releasing trapped emotions and clearing limiting beliefs.

She received three grants from the Lloyd Symington Foundation to present unique and creative approaches to grief, trauma and loss. She spoke at the Lloyd Symington Foundation-sponsored International Conference at Commonweal, which was featured in Bill Moyer's *Healing and The Mind.*

An award-winning filmmaker, Dr. Peticolas produced a 3-part documentary series, *Secrets of Life and Death.* Her films are screened in university classrooms throughout the United States, Canada, Australia and New Zealand. She is a featured author in the best-selling anthology *Breaking Barriers*, in which she chronicles her awakening to her life purpose during the deaths of her parents.

Email: mp@secretsoflifeanddeath.com
Phone: 510-529-4806
Website: https://www.secretsoflifeanddeath.com
https://www.facebook.com/secretsoflifeanddeath
https://www.linkedin.com/in/michellepeticolas/
https://twitter.com/secretsofnow
https://www.youtube.com/channel/UCpLeJ9ZBjETCqcmVkRPBtCg
https://www.pinterest.com/secretsofdeath/
https://instagram.com/michellepeticolas

DISCOVER THE VOICE OF YOUR SOUL
BY SOPHIE ROUMEAS

October 10, 2018

It seems that I arrived at 2. And I left at 12. Twelve, this is the end time of my appointment today. 2 is the number of people who were in my body. I left well at 12, but I was alone. He had to do an extraction. He, this is the therapist called The Wizard. A very black name for a very bright person. His light, he certainly owes it to his personal development and his mastering in Chinese and Tibetan medicine, put into practice and associated with other modalities well-connected. A curious mixture of acupuncture, with energetic and "magic" hands that practice a repairing surgery of the invisible. **In other words, those who need to see to believe may go their way.** My way stopped one day, thanks to the synchronicity for those who sometimes keep their noses in the air, where the wind leads them. Two years ago, I asked my intuition to find an acupuncturist. So, when your steps lead you one day to park by chance in front of a Chinese medicine center, with the doctor watering the flowers right in front of your car, you take the time to smile and to make an appointment with destiny, sorry, with the doctor!

I love when my mind catches words and puts them in shape with a hint of humor. It saves me time. Maybe to keep my mind present and not dissociated, after all, in the space of one hour, I went from 2 to 1. A single Sophie in my body, in my emotions, in my mind. It seems like I had a pact with my sister. We shared the space of my existence to save our mother from an emotional drowning. It is well known that children always want to save their parents. At all costs. Even at the cost of their own freedom. The Wizard shared with me that for 45 years we were discreetly mixed with my sister's spirit, unconsciously I would say, like a chain to my left ankle. Like African women with their anklets, to look pretty, and maybe not to forget History. I'll have to ask him more about this metaphor. **So, 45 years that I walk with an invisible bracelet waiting for someone to notice and release this link.**

Because my sister is not me. Yes, her name is Sophie. Yes, my parents wanted her. But Sophie died 18 months before I was born. Too early. The heart not enough formed. Not to say malformed. 47 years ago.

My mother never saw her daughter's body after the operation. My father and the medical team did not feel right to let her see the baby. No body, no funeral, no place after her death. And a great sorrow for this woman, my mother, who made them parents. Subsequently, our neurotic family life masked that they had loved each other "normally" for a time. Something after that drama had to break some pieces of my parents' heart.

But life goes on. It is as if things are resuming to their normal course; again people make love, and a small piece of soul is incarnated nine months after the embrace of the bodies. This baby is full-term, heart is formed, it is a girl—we will call her Sophie. In tribute to the one who was not born. That Sophie is me. It seems like I was a happy and chubby baby. Indeed, in a picture, two blue balls for the eyes and a Bibendum body dressed in a blue-striped white suit. A therapist told me that the space of a mother who lost her child, especially her first, is not the most colorful. I understand why, living both in an apartment with my mother after their divorce with my father—I was 5 years old, I was doing the "show" by tumbling down with my dolls and singing around the living room table, trying to bring a smile to my mother's frozen face and a spark of life to her eyes.

From my perception, I have never been able to satisfy my mother, from all my childhood and my teenage years to my voice that was not sharp enough, my belly not flat enough. And this memory, hearing sometimes before people came home, "*I hope you have something interesting to say*." These are things we do not forget easily. So, when I finally learned at the corner of an adult conversation that there had been a Sophie before me, everything had to light up in my child's head. I could turn on the light on the shadow of these behaviors. I think that's where I started connecting with the people of the Other Side. As I was a kind of daydreaming child, already cataloged "distracted, head in the moon," it certainly facilitated the process in my child's subconscious to get this girl from Beyond who could make my mother happy.

Even today, I learn to receive that I can be appreciated for who I am. And I am vigilant not to feel unconsciously obliged to fill with my presence someone sad because of absence. I also became good to feel the ideal partner for others. Even in my love stories where another was better than me. "Self-sabotage," the Wizard called it this morning. But of course. Even this book bought years ago to understand the imposter syndrome. One day, people may discover me different than who I am. For me, I would have waited years before hearing my inner voice whispering the words "self-sabotage," to raise awareness and solve it; if it did not prevent me from living beautiful things in my life, to perform acts of love, to give life to my two wonderful sons, to make various studies, the backstory of my life was colored with this recurring symptom. Like a perfume that would have permeated my clothes.

However, despite my efforts to transform this link energetically (some would name it "cell memory"), or symbolically, alone in the mountain to represent my family with candles, crying and rehabilitating the missing one so present by her silent absence—**the healing path became powerful when I finally wisely agreed not to be able to achieve all by myself.** Life places on our paths multitudes of signs that we are free to perceive or not, according to our consciousness in the present.

People like you and me dedicate their lives to facilitating people like you and me to find their path of inner freedom. All on the same primordial ocean, interactions never crossed by coincidence. This morning, the universe will have worked to get me ready for my appointment: 3 days before, I met another group of souls who animated my own systemic family constellation. The theme I chose was in resonance with today: "bring more peace to my family system, and bring my projects into light." The group circle showed in front of my eyes, the drama of this little girl born dead and the immense sadness of her mother, with the repercussions that this tragedy would have on our family. And indeed, our home was infused by the progressive disconnection of my parents as a couple, the emotional distance of my mother after she lost her own mother when I was 22 months old, the refusal of another child, my first brother, who nevertheless was born in the family chaos, but who finally died of an accident 38 years later. All these destinies deviated from light, more or less tragically, for at least one common reason: not recognizing soon enough souls in pain and not knowing how to cure them.

Parents, if one of your children seems regularly absent, in his/her thoughts, out of reality more frequently than "normal," ask yourself, or a professional, if there is perhaps a dissociation disorder. We can dissociate ourselves from reality for various reasons, go to a missing person from the Other Side, in solidarity with a parents, a sad or depressed family member, often during unfulfilled bereavement, replace unconsciously a denied or excluded person—behaviors made unconsciously for echoing well-kept family secrets for the "good of all"; in short, embodying invisible, unconscious family loyalties, which underlie daily acts in a more or less scuttled way. Usually, dissociation disorder, even more associated with self-sabotage, does not disappear alone and can have repercussions such as difficulty in demonstrating concrete actions for oneself, an ability to remain in the shadow, an inability to create a personal and authentic life scenario.

My message to convey at this moment, is to bring your attention to your family tree. Dare to ask questions to those alive, to voice the places taken, not taken, left, denied, to feel finally at your own good place. I thought for years that I was the eldest of my siblings, while in fact I am the second. And it suits me like that. While gradually finding my own consciousness, I also honor that my parents gave me life. **Truly thanking my mother and my father from my heart, I started to connect my soul's voice to share my gifts, to be at service with brilliance.**

Is it surprising, my sister would certainly be born to my exact opposite in Chinese medicine, in a sign of Water, I who am from Earth? Yes, everything is information; sometimes our bodies store information like stones, waiting to be taken into account. In my case, I had to release some crystals in my kidneys with conventional therapy before to give birth to my second son. Then, with complementary therapy, my body learned how to transform these crystal stones, so that I access my inner garden hidden behind them.

This morning, during the session, I yawned, flinched, closed my eyes, opened my eyes, searched for my breath, looked for the Wizard's gaze, sought the path of the Feel to allow my inner rebirth. Distinct from my sister, with respect and gratitude for our secret cohabitation of souls.

I share these facts to testify that instead of living as if this life was not really ours, we should find support and guidance. **If there is an inheritance that I wish to bequeath to my children, that's the self-confidence, their right beyond duty, to meet happiness, to feel "enough" and enjoy exploring life that they then contribute by blossoming naturally, without taking it as a toll or ultimately a burden during their time on earth.**

Therapies seeking to heal the Tree of Life have a bright future. All the better. Our world is deeply in need of finding a more ecological collective nature. To reintegrate one's genuine life trajectory, that's why **I became a therapist for 6 years. I tend to help people lift the veils on their sleeping memory with a mix of psycho-corporeal and cognitive practices, those that resonated on my own path. As individual sessions, group workshops, proved a common link between the people I facilitate; it eventually created my motto: *Let's Voice Your Soul!***

It is 3:30 pm; everything is fine. I put down my pen, the sun continues its trajectory, the wind slips into the hair and makes the leaves dance. Some walk alone or in pairs, others have a drink on the terrace of cafes; the world is not at peace everywhere. But for now, I enjoy the harmony and the light of the moment. I feel unified, pacified in my body, in balance between individual and collective consciousness. **By joining my voice to those of my co-authors, I want to bring my lighting to untie certain knots of destinies. So that you, I, us, we all step into the Brilliance.**

Tips to Help You Voice Your Soul:

1. **To Voice your Soul, you need first to hear your Voice.** Do you know that a few minutes of meditation a day is like showering your mind, your emotions? 7 minutes is the time it takes for the mind to calm down and center. After 12 minutes, the body begins to shed stress hormones; we gradually return from an automatic reaction mode to a mode of being and doing in consciousness. Your inner silence offers then a space to hear your Inner Voice (ultimately your intuition ♥).
2. **Sometimes your Voice may seem to be chaotic, specifically in hard or challenging time**. A very good friend of yours would be Nature. Walk barefoot as often as possible. At least walk 5 minutes a day near trees or water. And use your senses to feel nature. It would ground you and let your Being infuse with natural wisdom of the earth.
3. **If you find difficult to connect your authentic voice,** you may want to use the extraordinary tool of "systemic family constellation": you will be helped to find for what or who (by hidden loyalty to an absent, a dead one, a denied one) you hold your voice, actions, and joy back. There is a natural and universal order of life that manifests in existence by feeling in harmony in our family lineage and in our daily creativity. In this spirit, dare to write a letter to each of your parents to say thank you.
4. **Create your Life Board Vision**. By voicing your needs and dreams in words and images, you would be surprised by the efficiency of your intentions. If you want to meet your divine lover, don't write his/her size or weight, but speak the language of emotions; what would you like to feel with him/her? Positive emotions are key to setting intentions. And then, trust the echo of the universe. Yes, you are significant as well as the creator of your reality!
5. **In your Vision Board there may be the mission that your Soul chose** by birthing in your present life. It's quite crystal clear at the very beginning, but when we incarnate in a body it is said that we "lose memory" for a time. Is it what you feel? Go back to your roots. Do self-hypnosis or practice daily meditation with the intention to meet your inner child: what he/she dreamt earlier or went through is very often the soil of our initial mission, the reason for voicing our soul. Even if you don't feel it yet, you are part of the magic partition of the universe.
6. **Dare to ask for guidance when you feel stuck or without inspiration.** There are as many good reasons to go to a facilitator/therapist as the number of barriers that we put between our natural Brilliance, our aspirations, our Soul, and our reality. To be accompanied is a natural

part of existence. Let's find your mindful formula to **voice your soul and Step into the Brilliance**! You are welcome.

Sophie Roumeas

Mindful Therapy facilitator, Coach in mindfulness, Innovation consultant and product developer.

Attentive with people—some say sometimes that I see in them what they do not always perceive themselves.

In my first "life," I encountered personal and professional challenges that gradually damaged my capacity to voice my needs and desires. It led me to explore several techniques and solutions; I decided then to become a facilitator for change and to help people to voice themselves. It became my motto: ***Let's Voice Your Soul!***

We tailor a unique Mindful Formula with my clients, to manifest transformation and ultimately live with joy: the process of coaching is mixed à la carte with Ericksonian hypnosis, systemic constellations, energetic tools, and past life regression therapy.

I also facilitate workshops (systemic for organizations, stress management, innovation).

In 2016, I created **Alpes Meditation (AM)** to share mindfulness as a cognitive tool and a ritual for conscious living.

Since its inception, **AM** has been providing classes to individuals, health leagues, businesses and families, as we believe that mindfulness should be accessible to as many people as possible, regardless of age.

Collaborating with companies, **AM Innovation** is now a catalyst for products and services that serve corporate "Wellbeing and Innovation."

In daily life, I am partner, mother of two amazing sons, woman, sister, daughter, a friend and a facilitator for life change. I love to explore cultures through human interactions, art and nature, and as much put myself **at the service of people in search of resources**!

Email Address: sophie.roumeas@gmail.com
Phone Number: +33 683 318 914
Website: www.sophieroumeas.com
Facebook page(s):
https://www.facebook.com/SophieRoumeas2
https://www.facebook.com/pg/mindfulcandle/services
https://www.facebook.com/sophie.roumeas1/
LinkedIn Page: http://linkedin.com/in/sophie-rouméas-33b60261
Twitter handle: https://twitter.com/aminovation
Other Social Media Channels:
www.alpesmeditation.com
www.mindfulcandle.com

SECTION 3:

Step Into Your Brilliance & Shine!

LIVING LIFE WITH PASSION & PURPOSE
BY NINA HEIKKILA

When we least expect it, life can throw us a curveball. **The sudden loss of a job can be devastating, but it is also an opportunity to step into your greatness, shine your light, and start living your life on purpose.**

A few years ago, I could have written a long list of the reasons preventing me from quitting my job and pursuing my dreams, like losing a stable paycheck and receiving criticism from others.

Sitting in my office one day, I found myself struggling to breathe. I was having an anxiety attack. As tears ran down my face, I asked myself how I had ended up sacrificing my passion for a paycheck and feeling so defeated by life. At that moment, I heard a voice inside me say, *That's enough, it's time to leave!* But my mind was suddenly flooded with questions like: *How am I going to pay my bills and support my family?*

And that's when I chose not to listen to my inner wisdom telling me I was meant to do something greater with my life. Two months later, I was laid off. When the universe shook up my reality, I knew it was an opportunity to change the course of my life, and there was no better time to ask:

What have I got to lose?

My battle with childhood leukemia changed my life. Instead of a carefree childhood, my days alternated between going to school and long stays in the hospital. When I went to school, I was often teased because I had lost my hair. I grew older, but my low levels of confidence and self-esteem left me drifting further away from my childhood dreams. For ten years, I ended up changing jobs, going around in circles, and feeling stuck.

After doing some soul-searching, I came to the point where I asked the universe, *Why am I here?*

It was then that I realized that everything I had been through WAS meaningful and significant! Starting from an early age, I had faced challenges and overcome them. After that, I made a vow to live a life that had meaning and purpose.

The Life You Were Meant to Live

If you have heard your inner voice telling you that you are not living up to your potential and you are meant to do something more meaningful, then **it is time to step into your greatness.**

Is there something in your childhood that you have always regretted giving up? What is stopping you from authentically being who you came into this lifetime to be?

Playing small limits your true potential and stops you from sharing your unique gifts with the world. At some point on our journey, we choose to change the way that we have been doing things. As our awareness increases, we desire to live a more meaningful life, and we realize how living in fear has limited our experiences in the past. **From that point on, we can stop making choices out of fear and decide to make them out of love instead.**

The thought of switching careers brought about the fear that I didn't have the right qualifications for a position in another field. I felt unworthy, and that I was too old to change careers. **These judgments hadn't come**

from anyone else, but I allowed myself to believe them.

The fear of trying something different and failing limited my perspective of the situation and the opportunities available to me. I kept trying to reinvent the wheel by pursuing the same types of jobs and expecting a different outcome. Finally, the universe had no other option than a great big upheaval of my life.

What drove me forward was the fear of going back to doing what I had done in the past, which was far greater than the fear of taking action.

When I lost my job, it was a pivotal moment, I chose to forge a different path, to beat the odds, and to create the life that I wanted.

After faithfully reciting affirmations, meditating, and stating my goals for eight weeks, I experienced a shift in my mindset. I had started to believe that I could achieve anything that I wanted. And after three months, I manifested my ideal job, working in the film industry as a set designer.

One of the tell-tale signs that, somewhere along the way, we stopped paying attention to our desires can be described as feeling "lost," due to a lack of clarity about what we should be doing and which direction we're supposed to go. Other clues are:

- Your choices are driven by fear, and you constantly worry about the future.

- Knowing you have unlimited potential waiting to be unleashed, but you never have the opportunity to do so.

- Other people see you as the definition of success, but you feel there is something missing.

Consciously choosing the kind of work you would enjoy doing will begin to align with your purpose. Doing so gives you a greater sense of stability in the world, as you no longer live according to someone else's expectations, or feel as though life is just happening to you...

When you live on purpose, you live life on a deeper and more meaningful level. Your passion ignites, your goals in life become clear, and your inner guidance begins directing you, telling you what actions you must take next.

The Power of Purpose

What has stopped your from pursuing your goals in the past?

Throughout history, every person that changed how things were done was faced with numerous obstacles and challenges. At some point, they all asked themselves:

- How strong is my fear of failure?
- How strong is my fear of being judged?
- How strong is my fear of the unknown?
- How strong is my fear of things staying the way they are today?

How strong is your desire to change the course of your life and your destiny?

If you allow it to, FEAR will stop you from pursuing your dreams and living a life filled with joy, abundance, and purpose.

It's your burning desire and your relentless determination that will motivate you to do whatever it takes to realize your dreams. And your passion will create the momentum that is required to overcome obstacles along the way.

Have faith in your limitless potential and your ability to achieve your goals.

Becoming Who You Were Meant to Be

The universe has a way of guiding you back to your highest path when your parents, teachers, or society, may have led you astray.

Ignoring the signs from the universe, telling you to change your course, will keep you repeating the same patterns, eventually followed by a breakdown, a breakthrough, and a spiritual awakening.

Think of a true awakening as a spark that ignites your passion, inspiring you to follow your heart and pursue your dreams and goals.

Your Inner Voice

We are often led to believe that personal fulfillment and success are achieved by owning luxury cars, large homes, and a certain annual income. But even after we obtain these things, we may feel unfulfilled and wonder what is missing from our lives.

When we begin the process of self-discovery and find out what gives us pleasure, sparks our passion, and fills us with joy, we hit the jackpot! We finally uncover what we are meant to do in life.

Trust me, you can't miss the giant arrow with flashing lights pointing to the path that will lead to the life that you truly desire.

Questions to help clarify your purpose include:

- What kind of person do I want to be? (list the characteristics you value)
- What brings me the most joy, happiness, and fulfillment?
- If money wasn't a factor, what would I love to do?
- If I knew that I could not fail, what would I do?
- What kind of legacy do I want to leave behind?

Signs That You Have Found Your Passion and Purpose

Write down the details about the kind of person want to be, the kind of life you intend to live, and the things that you intend to do. This creates the very definition of your life purpose. When you read it, it will stir up a powerful response within you and make you smile. You'll internally respond, *Yes, that's me!*

When you experience high levels of excitement and get so caught up in the process that you completely lose track of time, your inner voice will tell you, *Yes! Keep doing more of that!*

You also have:

1. Absolute clarity on the things that are most fulfilling and meaningful to you.

2. A crystal-clear vision about how you would like to share your talents and abilities with the world.

3. A clear knowing about the role that you intend to play in the world and a strong sense of your mission.

Your highest path is a "knowing," more than it is a destination.

Living in the Flow

You may have experienced a magical time where everything that you wanted and needed just seemed to show up in your life at the perfect moment. This is the mystical state of "flow," which the Taoist refer to as an effortless life, living in harmony with the universe.

We come into this lifetime with an internal compass, which spiritual teachers refer to as intuition. The ideas and nudges that we experience point us in the right direction and inspire us to take the necessary actions that lead to achieving our goals.

Getting into the "flow" means releasing all fear and doubt and allowing a higher power to take over, trusting that the universe will always deliver what you really want in life.

**"Let yourself be silently drawn
by the strange pull of what you really love.
It will not lead you astray."**
— RUMI

In any situation, we have the power to choose our thoughts and actions. Accepting responsibility for all aspects of our lives is not an easy thing to do, but it is a necessary step in our growth and development. The paths we chose to take were the ones that were required to learn our biggest lessons.

We are always under so much pressure to be perfect, but there are no mistakes in this life. If you took a risk and didn't achieve what you wanted, give yourself some credit; it takes courage to reach for the brass ring.

Sometimes, when things don't work out, it wasn't in your highest interest, and the universe is showing you that there are other ways to achieve what you want. We often don't consider this, and we tend to get upset and lose our motivation or give up. But we have a mind with the capability to reflect on our past experiences and to learn from them. This is how we grow as human beings.

Who You Really Are

Your purpose in life is to align with your desires, to consistently take steps towards your goals, and to believe that everything will all work out for the best.

Over the course of our lives, our internal stories place a ceiling on our success and happiness. **But the truth is that we are spiritual beings with unlimited potential, and deep within us lies our unique brilliance, waiting to express itself and shine out into the world.**

You don't have to have a near-death experience, or any kind of life-changing event, to start changing your life. At some point, the universe will send an opportunity that calls out to you, and your job is to stand up and say, "Yes!"

Every day, my faith in myself and my belief in the invisible force called the universe help me overcome the fear of taking action. In the past three years, I have accomplished goals the old me never could have imagined for myself. I have also become more comfortable when facing uncertainty, knowing that every moment holds infinite possibilities. I trust that whatever comes up is exactly what is needed to get me to where I want to go, and that I have all the tools I need to overcome challenges along the way.

When you surrender your fears, pursue your passion, and stay open to the opportunities that appear to you in the present moment, magic happens. Serendipity lights the way, and the path that leads to everything you want unfolds before you.

Relax and enjoy your adventure in a world that is full of possibility.

Right now, the power is already within you. And so, I encourage you:

To be bold,
To take the road less travelled,
To expect miracles.

Become a shining example of what **CAN BE DONE,** inspiring others to do the same.

"And the day came when the risk it took to stay tight in the bud was greater than the risk it took to blossom."
–Anaïs Nin

Nina Heikkila

Nina is an Intuitive Spiritual Success & Abundance Coach
Certified Law of Attraction Coach
Inspirational Speaker & Author of *Leaving the Matrix*
Nina works with women on a spiritual level, teaching them how to work with their Intuition & the Law of Attraction to achieve their highest potential.

(403) 975-1861
ninaloacoach@gmail.com
https://livinginabundanceyyc.com/
Facebook: Living in Abundance yyc

SPEAK YOUR BRILLIANCE
BY CYNTHIA STOTT

Miss Wiggles. This was my nickname in my college speech class because my whole body shook, my lip quivered, and I could barely get my words out. I was terrified!

After college, I joined the Federal Reserve Bank of San Francisco. Within a few weeks of working there, I found out that they had a Toastmasters Club, where I could practice my speaking in a supportive environment. They met on the same floor as the cafeteria where I ate every day, and the FED would even pay my dues! I wanted to join, but was too terrified to set foot into a meeting, even as a guest, for 13 years.

I lived with 5 strong phobias for almost 40 years of my life. Speaking, visibility, dancing in public and spiders were my worst fears—I was pretty much afraid of everything. My college roommate called me a "Wuss," a 1990s term for scaredy-cat. She wasn't mean, just truthful.

I have since overcome these fears, most have become my passion:

1. **Speaking:** I have won numerous speech competitions and am an International Speech Coach.
2. **Visibility:** I have over 30,000 followers in more than 140 countries and am a Social Media Influencer.
3. **Heights:** I've done a 17-story bungee jump and LOVED IT!
4. **Dancing**: I'm known internationally for my dancing on stage.
5. **Spiders:** NOT my passion. However, I no longer fear them and think the little ones are cute.

What Changed? How did I go from a total scaredy-cat to what some people have called fearless?

April 3, 2003—the day my whole life changed. I had met my soulmate in college. Nerds who found chemistry in the chemistry study room, we remained "honeymooners" long after we were married. One of our friends said, "I thought that kind of love only existed in the movies, until I met you two." I joked that 2003 was our bad luck year—13 years together and 7 years of marriage. If we could get through this year, we could get through anything.

We didn't.

I came home from a business trip on that fateful day and Dean (my beloved husband) had died in his sleep. He was 38 years old. He had sleep apnea. I knew it was serious, but I had no idea that it could take him at such a young age.

I was devastated. I cried for three weeks straight. I cried so much I became dehydrated. I literally had no more tears. I would drink water and then would cry some more. My father-in-law joked that I should "cut out the middle man" and just pour the water over my head. I laughed, and cried, and laughed and then cried, then drank water and cried some more.

I never realized the depth of grief that was possible until that day. I felt like a big part of me died with Dean.

Somehow I got through those first few months and then years. To help me cope, I joined a yoga group to learn to meditate and develop a deeper relationship with myself. Before Dean's death, I was the world's worst meditator, my body would flop like a fish, and I just couldn't sit still. A mental health professional told me that I was one of the rare people who is "allergic" to meditation. I wasn't. I just needed a method that worked for me. Now I'm an expert meditator and teach others to meditate and connect with their inner selves in deep and powerful ways.

In those early days of grief, my yoga master was able to help me to stop the cycle of crying and dehydration. The yoga master said, "Your bladder is tight." I had no idea what that meant but I agreed to let her help me. Whatever she did caused me to go to the bathroom every 20 minutes for the next 24 hours. After that, I cried—a lot—but never to the point of dehydration.

I went to one of their self-discovery workshops. It was on what would have been our 8th wedding anniversary. I figured getting to know myself better would be the best way to spend this difficult day.

The instructor said, "Your life is a blank sheet of paper on which you can draw a new picture every day. What do you want?"

"I want COURAGE!" I didn't want to live my life in fear anymore.

It took lots of mediation, healing, and connecting with myself, but suddenly my fears started disappearing! I first noticed that my fear of heights disappeared. My fear had been so bad that when I went to the Seattle Space Needle with Dean, I had hugged the wall and wouldn't even approach the window, and it was closed!

I was hiking back down from Airport Mesa in Sedona, Arizona and I suddenly realized that my fear of heights was GONE. I had been on top of that mountain—with sheer cliffs 1,500 feet down—meditating and doing yoga postures in pure bliss and relaxation. It freaked me out for a moment. Who am I? In that moment, my identity of myself began to shift.

I worked through my grief, gaining more and more of myself along the way.

Then something else happened that changed the trajectory of my life.

In December 2006, I got my mission, a calling that was laid on my heart. I had become a part-time yoga, martial arts, and brain education instructor through this same group. My yoga master suggested that we yoga instructors go home and meditate and ask what our 6-month, 1-year, and 5-year goals might be.

As I sat down to meditate, I realized I didn't know where to begin. God asked me, "What do you want?" I could think of a number of things, but all seemed kind of silly in this profound moment. **God asked me, "What do you want more than anything?" With tears in my eyes I said, "Peace on Earth. True peace and harmony in a world where I really want to live."**

As I dove deeper into my heart, two powerful revelations came out. I heard God say, "You will live on the Big Island of Hawaii." Wow, I LOVE Hawaii! **Then I heard what put trepidation in my whole body and being. "You will create a corporate retreat center and bring CEOs and executives to work on their vision that will be win-win for themselves, their employees, their bottom line and the world."**

Wow! I was so overwhelmed by this vision. The first words out of my mouth were, "I'd better get to Toastmasters!" I knew I needed to speak well in order to engage and enroll these CEOs and executives. I joined 5 months later.

I received an email about a Toastmasters World Champion of Public Speaking that was coming to my region. He was a stand-up comedian and he was going to teach us how to bring humor to our speeches. I knew that in order to reach people and enroll them in doing things differently, I needed to have humor in my arsenal.

"How can I go? I'm supporting my 89-year-old mother who fell and broke her hip. I'm seeing A *Christmas Carol* with my friend that night and it ends at 9 pm!" Then the face of my club president popped in my head. With his beautiful French accent he said, "But, it is YOUR DREAM!"

I headed on the 119.2-mile trip at 10 pm on that stormy December night. I passed 3 accidents along the way, encountered ice going over the Santa Cruz mountains, and arrived at my hotel after midnight.

My yoga master had said, "Volunteer. Don't ask for what, just volunteer." When the trainer asked for volunteers, I forced my hand up." I kept moving to the back of the line of the 7 volunteers on stage. While number

6 was taking his turn speaking to the 300-person audience, I started to see a black curtain. Remember the old televisions that faded to black with a large circle growing smaller? That's what I saw and knew that I was about to pass out. All I could think was, "Breathe, Cynthia. Breathe."

I didn't pass out. I immediately marched myself to the back of the room and bought $1,000 of his programs, CDs and DVDs. I knew I needed expert training and support if I was to carry out my big scary vision.

Since then, I have supported hundreds of speakers all around the world to speak their truth. The truth of who they are and stand in the beautiful gift that they are to the world.

Knees knocking, voice quivering, and even swearing in frustration, I've helped them to dive deep into their hearts and who they are to pull out their authentic message and deliver it to the world.

Speak. Why? Because **YOUR PEOPLE ARE WAITING FOR YOU! In fact, they are probably praying for someone like you—with your talents, skills, passion and yes, even your wounds or the difficult things you have experienced in your life.**

There are two sides to the coin. If you have a calling or message that has been laid on your heart, then you have people who are also calling to you. **In fact, if you're willing to show up for them, they will call forth your deepest messages and gifts.**

One woman came to my Speaker Boot Camp so frustrated she was dropping "F-Bombs," so angry at me for "making" her do this. By the end of the day, everything changed. I taught the class my speech ritual for protection and grounding. It is designed to put you in your "Angel Space," a state of connection with your higher self and protection using the tools of Love, Light, and Power.

She gave her speech from her full Angel Power. Her eyes were sparkling, and her face was aglow, like a pregnant woman. Afterward, she approached me with her hand on her heart and tears in her eyes and said, "Cynthia, I never knew how much my message meant to me." She surely had people waiting for her powerful message.

Another client saw an amazing future for herself in a private Future Gazing session, a deep guided session with me where your highest self reveals more of what's possible for you. She was speaking to about 400 people, offering a program costing $50,000 per person. She watched in meditation as many of them clamored to sign-up. She was understandably overwhelmed with this revelation of what was possible for her as a speaker. I had her "read" the offer she was handing out in this vision. Now, she has the point-by-point features of this sought-after program on a recording. She immediately gave herself a $500 raise and has been growing into it ever since. Her programs went from $1,500 to $15,000 and above. She truly is the answer to her people's prayers.

Another one of my speaker clients was practicing for an audition. I pointed out that the community leaders for whom she was auditioning were some of her most ideal clients. I taught her techniques to engage and connect so that her ideal clients would easily sign up. She called me after the audition and said, "Cynthia, I would have never believed it. They all signed up!" Her people were truly waiting for her.

What I would share with my past self to encourage me on my journey is, "Everything's going to be okay." And so, I share this wisdom with you: everything is going to be okay and know that your people are waiting for you.

If you have a message or calling that's been laid on your heart, don't wait:

- SPEAK, as often as you can. Knees knocking, voice quivering, SPEAK.
- When you're afraid or can't take another step. BREATHE, put your mind at your FEET and wiggle your TOES. It changes your brain chemistry and outcome.
- GET EXPERT SUPPORT. You are not meant to do this alone.
- DON'T GIVE UP. Your people are WAITING for YOU!

Cynthia Stott

Cynthia Stott is a best-selling author, International Speaker Coach and Global Visibility Influencer. She was terrified of public speaking and visibility but now empowers entrepreneurs and speakers to overcome fears, speak, be visible, and make money doing what they love. She believes Your People are WAITING for YOU!

With her first free call in 2012, she used a Facebook event to grow her tribe by more than one an hour from 6 countries. Now she has over 30,000 followers from over 140 countries on Twitter, Facebook, and LinkedIn.

Cynthia has had a life-long passion to make a difference. In her 18-year career at the Federal Reserve Bank, she developed a program to detect pricing discrimination in auto lending and changed the way banks and auto dealerships do business. She didn't find out about the national impact she had made for 10 years! Cynthia believes that, when you follow your heart with passion and purpose, you change the world—even in ways you will never know.

Cynthia has been called an "Embodied Visionary" who is changing the way you can impact the world and do business online and in our own backyard.

Your People are WAITING for YOU! The question is, are you ready for them?

Media Links:

Email: Programs@CynthiaStott.com
Phone/Text: 415.298.7306
Website: www.CynthiaStott.com
Facebook Pages:
www.facebook.com/cynthia.stott.18
www.facebook.com/TheSpeakerSummit/
Twitter: @CynthiaStott or www.Twitter.com/CynthiaStott
LinkedIn: www.LinkedIn.com/in/CynthiaStott

IT'S SHOWTIME! IT'S TIME TO SHINE!
BY JANICE L. EDWARDS

"Janice Edwards, it's show time; it's time to shine!"

Those lyrics from my television show's new theme song made me gasp the first time I heard them. To me, it was like a love letter from God delivered via the genius of recording artist and composer Ron Scott, singers Bridget Marie Anderson Lopes and Jivoni Paul Jordan, guitarist Rob Lopes, and mixed by Sean Brophy and Steve Glazer.

When we discussed a theme song for my show Janice Edwards' Bay Area Vista, I didn't imagine one with my name in it. It heralded an opportunity to shine in an even brighter way. Like many people I know, there is often a dance between my introvert and my extrovert: appreciation of the light shining on achievements and enjoyment of the moments of retreat and renewal. The boldness of the title of our book, Step into Your Brilliance, speaks to a level of confidence and comfort that for me has been hard-won and is preciously nurtured at this juncture of life.

Regarding the theme song, Ron Scott told me he thought of it the night he saw me working on scripts for the show we were shooting at the San

Jose Jazz Summer Fest. After MC-ing on the main stage and getting the festival-goers pumped up for Chris Botti's amazing performance, he said, "this girl has been working hard both behind the scenes as a producer and out front on camera for years; we've got to put her name in the song!" **When the song was played at the CreaTiVe Awards in 2018 where our show, Janice Edwards' Bay Area Vista: Snoop Youth Football League and Felton Institute won an award, it was a joyful and surreal moment.** One I wished my mother could have shared.

* * *

Her breathing had become more labored. Her eyes, though focused on me, were barely open. I was stroking her forehead and using my other hand to hold hers. While I had been talking to her earlier, I stopped, alarmed at her obvious discomfort. "Should we move her?" I asked the nurse. Silently, with full eyes, the nurse shifted her on the bed. My beloved mother looked at me with widened eyes; a deep sigh escaped her throat, and she took her last breath.

It was 1:51 pm on the first Saturday in July. It was a lovely sunny day outside; nothing in the atmosphere reflected the earthquake in my soul.

As I contemplate my life both before and ever since Mommy's passing seven and a half years ago, I am so glad that she had an opportunity to see me shine, and I believe that in another dimension, her fierce advocacy for me and pride in my work continues to inform the purpose of what God has graciously allowed me to do on this planet. I believe that both she and my cherished father are reunited in heaven and continually petition on my behalf. I am the only child of a father who was the first in his immediate family to earn a law degree and of a mother who was the first, and remains the only, member of her family to earn a Ph.D. **Their desire for me was to be a good person and to fulfill my highest potential.**

I am a talk show host and executive producer of an award-winning show, Janice Edwards' Bay Area Vista, a show that I launched 17 years ago while working at NBC Bay Area in the San Francisco Bay Area and have produced independently for a decade. (Though I say "independently," I have an amazing team of production angels, sponsors, and friends as collaborators who have made it possible. My show has aired on ION-TV, KCSM-TV, CreaTV, and KRON, through Edwards Unlimited productions).

I am a member of the 2019 class of Black Legends of Silicon Valley in the News and Documentary category, an Emmy nominee, and the President and CEO of my production company, Edwards Unlimited. My career and life credits include work as talk show host and executive producer, update anchor and producer, news writer, reporter, videographer, radio talk show host, community relations director, and actress; the stations at which I've worked include NBC Bay Area, CBS 5, KRON 4, ABC 7, KBHK, CreaTV, WSB, and KFAX Radio. **In earlier years, I sometimes lamented that there was no clear straight path for my career, but the more I understand about life, I see that many who seemed to have straight paths to me have had their share of curveballs.**

I sometimes joke that my career as a reporter started as narrator of The Nutcracker in first grade. At sixteen, I was co-host of a teen radio show; after graduating cum laude from Harvard, I left East Coast winters behind for sunny California and the graduate school journalism program at UC Berkeley. Acting highlights include sharing the stage with Anna Deveare Smith in Oakland Ensemble Theatre's two-woman show Sisters and portraying Mrs. Coretta Scott King at Stanford's Dr. Martin Luther King, Jr.'s Papers Project. Among hundreds of interviews conducted, highlights include Oprah Winfrey, Barack Obama (on his first book tour), Madeleine Albright, Dr. Deepak Chopra, Dr. Cornel West, Kevin Costner, Robin Williams, Rob Reiner, Chris Pine, Jane Pauley, Kerry Washington, Quincy Jones, Eartha Kitt, Della Reese, Robert Townsend, D. Channsin Berry, Annette Bening, Anna Faris, Josh Hutcherson, Snoop Dogg, Idris Elba, Marlee Matlin, Will Farrell, Howard E. Rollins, Jr, Viggo Mortenson, Rita Moreno, and Robert Redford, who complimented my interview style and jokingly invited me to accompany him on tour and ask questions. [https://youtu.be/GfcW3xDoAsg]

I am a prayer warrior, intercessor, and minister. I am a woman humbled by the joyful life I am privileged to live, full of rich relationships, and I am a woman forever transformed by both love and loss, tenderness and toxicity, compassion and cruelty, and God's amazing grace in my life. **If there is one thing I could have whispered to myself during the darkest hours, it is "trust God, keep moving forward and believe that your dreams will come true."**

I have been invited to share my talk **"Five Keys to Being the Star in the Talk Show of Your OWN Life" ™ on several occasions, and I'd like to**

share two of the keys with you now.

PREP FOR YOUR INNER CLOSE-UP

- With all the filters, selfie sticks, and HD video effects on phones, it's easy to create illusions and project desirable perceptions, but two old sayings remain true: "the eyes are the window of the soul" and "the eyes don't lie." If you want to shine and bask in the brilliance that is your birthright, you have to face both hard and soft truths about yourself and your life. It's popular to invite others to keep it real and face the hard truths about yourself and your life, but the soft truths—the whispers of your soul reminding you of your long-held dream—need to be nurtured to help you move forward in life. Forgive yourself and others as quickly as possible and hold onto your integrity. When you can look in the mirror and smile at yourself, when you fully accept and love who you see there, then it will shine through in your eyes; it will radiate from your countenance and your physical walk and your walk in life will reflect it.
- Never give up. My mother once gave me a copy of her favorite poster: it shows two frog legs kicking as they hang from a pelican's beak and the frog's hands around the pelican's neck. The frog's head is in the pelican's beak, and the caption reads, "Never Give Up!" Do a reality test for your goals and desires, and then if you are clear that you must continue with them, act in integrity and keep moving forward.
- Let your faith guide your way, and let that foundation undergird you and sustain you. As one in my inner circle shared, when he gets discouraged or down about life's losses and disappointments, he thinks about Jesus on the cross. "It reminds me of how much God loves me, and all of us, to sacrifice His Son. Think about that, even with whatever you go through, you talk about committed—He wants us more than anything!" Connect with those who remind you that you are loved and treasured. Jeremiah 29:11 is one of my favorite scriptures because it says that God's plans for us are to give us a future and a hope.

<u>CUT TOXIC GUESTS FROM THE ROSTER: DON'T LET THEM STAY ON YOUR COUCH</u>

- In the world of "reality television," the bad characters who cause the drama and the fights are considered the most entertaining to watch. The clips of an irate guest walking off the set will be replayed much more and often will get thousands more views than an uplifting interview focusing on sources of inspiration. Boorish, brutal communication and lies send the false message that the most outrageous people are the most powerful. It's a false narrative; don't let that kind of darkness eclipse your light. In the reality of my own life, I have found that eliminating the interactions that steal my peace have led to success and empowerment. Getting out of repetitive negative cycles and learning from those who have mastered successful living in an area has provided (and still provides) illumination along my path. Cultivating healthy relationships and being around nurturing family, friends and colleagues is critical. During times of illness and pain, I know it can feel especially uncomfortable to reach out when vulnerable, but those are the times when it is most important not to isolate. You have to strategize for your life and navigate with deft precision. Don't apologize for wanting to have as healthy a life experience as you can.
- Sometimes the toxic guests can even be thoughts in your head or emotions that take you on a rollercoaster ride that isn't fun and leaves you screaming. Feed your mind and spirit what they need to be strong, healthy, and connected to your vibrant inner core. Don't let a song on your playlist or the radio guide you into memories that do not serve you—delete it and replace it with one that reminds you of the highest good that you desire in life.
- Sometimes the toxic guests can be foods to which you are allergic but still crave. Do whatever you can to eliminate those as well and enjoy the freedom from them.
- If you worry that cutting toxic guests means you will have lots of time on air or on screen with no one else there, consider a monologue or going to break to provide a little time to regroup. Leaving the analogy for a moment, when you eliminate the drama and chaos that you can from your life, it can feel like an altered universe, but if you give yourself some time to adjust, yet keep moving forward, you will have new experiences that delight and surprise you. And before you know it, you will have new amazing guests sitting on your sofa.

Sometimes you will not be able to feel the call of destiny waiting for you on the other side of the challenging day and dark night that you face, but it is there. Know that your destiny is calling you forward

and it is often just on the other side of darkness. Right now, there are people you haven't even met yet who are counting on you to make it to the other side of the obstacle you see. Hopefully, you have people right there with you reminding you of how truly brilliant you are. Know that you are a radiant star and bring into your circle those (change from that to who eliminate "that") who will remind you of your brilliance. **Those people help remind you that in the show of your life, now, "it's showtime; it's your time to shine!"**

Janice Edwards

Janice Edwards is an award-winning talk show host and Emmy nominated producer, media coach, published author and an acclaimed contributor to community empowerment through media. She is the host and executive producer of Janice Edwards' Bay Area Vista, which made its broadcast debut on NBC Bay Area in 2002; the show features community leaders, celebrities, non-profit organizations, and compelling issues. Janice Edwards' Bay Area Vista is produced through Edwards Unlimited. Janice is President and CEO of Edwards Unlimited, her media company that produces high quality videos to help entrepreneurs, nonprofit organizations, and corporations share their business success and philanthropic vision with the world. Janice's impressive television credits include years at NBC Bay Area, KRON 4, KPIX, CreaTV, and KBHK-TV; her radio credits include KFAX and KPFA Radio.

Her more than 1200 interviews span a variety and include Barack Obama, Oprah Winfrey, Madeleine Albright, Rachel Maddow, Dr. Deepak Chopra, Robert Redford, John Travolta, Snoop Dogg, Jerry Seinfeld, Gloria Steinem, Iyanla Vanzant, Kerry Washington, Idris Elba, Chris Pine, Les Brown, Dr. Cornel West, Regina King and John Cena. Janice is a published co-author of the book ***Quality Angles.*** Recent honors include the 2019 Induction into the Black Legends of Silicon Valley Hall of Fame; 2018, 2015, 2012, and 2011 CreaTiVe TV Series Awards for *Janice Edwards' Bay Area Vista*; 2013 Trailblazer Award from the National Coalition of 100 Black Women San Francisco; 2013 Hometown Media Award to "Signature Silicon Valley," 2010 Emmy nomination, 2010 and 2011 nominations for Woman Entrepreneur of the Year, 2010 NAACP W.E. Dubois Award, and 2010 Community Service Award from the Alpha Kappa Alpha Sorority of Silicon Valley.

Janice's career in broadcasting began in Atlanta, Georgia, as co-host of a teen radio talk show. She continued to work in radio and to write for Spanish and English newspapers as an undergraduate at Harvard University and a graduate student at UC Berkeley School of Journalism. Before graduating cum laude from Harvard, she studied in Spain.

Website: thejaniceedwards.com
Facebook: Janice Edwards on Bay Area Vista
Twitter: Janice BA Vista
YouTube: tvjaniceedwards
Instagram: tvjaniceedwards
Email: care@thejaniceedwards.com

SAY YES TO YOUR CALLING AND SHINE!
BY REBECCA HALL GRUYTER

I couldn't believe the energy surrounding me in this enormous conference center—thousands of women gathering together. The crowd. The noise. The connection. The moment I was swept up in the crowd and pulled forward. Eventually finding my seat high in the bleachers. A hush falls over the sea of faces. Lights turn down and the stage lights turn on. The event is about to begin. Little did I know... I'm attending an event that would change my life, plant a seed in my heart, and show me a calling in my life to step forward and SHINE!

You always have the choice to say yes or no.

There were many times when I said no to my brilliance, when I heard what I was being called to do and chose not to do it. I will never forget one defining moment and the choice I made.

When I was 19 years old, I attended a Women of Faith Conference, where not hundreds but thousands of motivational speakers gathered.

All different shapes and sizes were there, one by one taking the stage to share their personal stories of abuse, hardship, tragedy, and struggle. I sat mesmerized by the power of their messages, how God had led them to use those things they did not choose to experience in order to help and encourage other women.

It suddenly came to me—what if MY story could be used for good? What if I could turn the destruction that happened in that house, that family, into something good?

"I know what I want to do with my life!"

As I left the conference, I could feel a surge of inspiration, hope, excitement flow through my body. This is it—I can do this! I rushed home and announced to my mom, "I know what I want to do with my life!" While she was excited for me, she said, "Rebecca, that's wonderful! That means you actually have to get up on a stage and speak."

"Oh-h-h . . ." I was shocked, horrified. I hadn't connected those very logical dots. Of course, that's what a motivational speaker does. I could feel a shrinking back and contraction inside me, all that expansion literally dying away.

Being visible in front of people seemed impossible. I felt my purpose calling to me, but I believed I could never do that: stand in front of others and speak. So, I made the choice to ignore the calling out of fear that I was not strong enough or able to do it. Who was I to stand before crowds of people and share my story? How could I ever encourage them to live their lives on purpose? I could barely stand in front of more than two people and say my name, let alone take the stage in front of a group. To survive in the abusive environment of my childhood, I had learned to stay below the radar; it was unsafe to be seen and heard. I was still carrying those fears with me, speaking up only with extreme fear and discomfort, knees shaking, throat closing up.

I now know that even though I said no at that time, the seed of my calling had been planted—I just wasn't ready yet. It meant that the seed just needed to send down stronger roots and grow a little bit more so that it could emerge at its right time. The seed was planted and buried; the dream and calling just needed a bit more time to grow deeper roots before it could emerge through the surface where others could see it.

The things we're called to do that make our heart sing don't really die if we don't say yes to them right away. They are there waiting for us to uncover and bring out our brilliance, step by step, one small success at a time. But we must keep our hearts open to hear our calling and all the possibilities before us along the way.

Brilliance often rises out of struggle

Struggle can be a huge gift in bringing our brilliance to light. It can create a hunger and desire to shift to something new and better, perhaps to face a fear so we can move beyond it. It may happen in large or little ways, our brilliance and gifts emerging little by little until we gain more momentum and courage to truly step into our brilliance and SHINE!

Some of my brilliance and gifting is that I'm willing to say yes if it could make a difference for another. The inspiration I felt that day at the conference was my calling to help other women by sharing my story. I wanted something good to come out of my pain and struggle—that it could actually be used for good by helping another. Saying yes has led me to all kinds of places frequently outside of my comfort zone! I'm willing to go there, to fall and stand up again, to learn and grow, and to share what I know.

It always comes back to my purpose of making a difference for someone else, which gives me the courage to step outside of my comfort zone even more, to bring it forward even more. I'm willing to feel the fear and step forward if it can help another. As life is not a solo journey, we can and need to walk beside each other.

How about you? What are some of your gifts/brilliance that rise up consistently in your life? What moves you forward? What would you love to share with others and have make a positive difference in their lives by your sharing?

I didn't know I had a gift for speaking until I started stepping into that space and trying it on to see how it felt, slowly expanding my story and the size of the stage. I have realized it was my struggles in childhood that give me the power and determination to try things and "dance" with my fears. I don't like being limited or held back. I never again want to be in a position where I am powerless and living in fear. Not that I had a choice as a child in an abusive situation, but, I could choose not to now as an adult! My struggles have turned into a gift toward bringing my brilliance forward. Motivating and inspiring me, reminding me how much freedom and choice I have now to live on purpose and with purpose. To share and SHINE!

I remember being so shy in high school. I moved from a private school to a new public school in my senior year. I was starting fresh; no one knew me. I knew I wanted to be less shy and better at connecting with people. So I asked myself the questions: "What if I could connect better with others? How might I go about it? What would it look like and feel like?" I made the decision to *act like* I was better at connecting with others. I observed what other people were doing, like making good eye contact, smiling at people, asking questions. I thought, "Well, I could do that."

So, by college, that person who could hardly whisper her name in front of people would walk right up to a table of students at lunchtime, smile, and say, "Hi. I'm Rebecca, and I'm working on my communications skills," as I would rather boldly start to sit down. "Is it okay if I sit with you?" They always let me join them and we had great authentic conversations. I loved it and the powerful connections that could be formed by leaning in and reaching out to others.

As I went through college, I even would deliberately choose a table that looked unfriendly or scary! I ended up meeting so many friends in all different groups and loving it. I don't know exactly what gave me the courage to do this, but I think that determination to be in my power, along with my love of truly connecting with others and bringing people together, is what carried me through. What I found is that we all are so much more alike than we think we are, at a core level and how we care about what really matters. Which, of course, nurtured the seed of my purpose to continue to grow.

Do you see how stepping into your brilliance can work? Step by step, here is how you can start planting and growing your own seed of purpose.

What if—?

You can start by asking yourself this question: "What if—?" What if I could make a difference? What if I could take a tiny step to speak in front of people? What if I say yes to a networking invitation? "What if—?" gives you an opportunity to try "it" on, whatever "it" may be for you.

This question gives you an opportunity to step into the experience of this new direction, idea, and possibility without having to fully commit to it yet. It's like you're trying it on for a moment, seeing how it fits and feels. Does it pull at your heart? Are you excited by it? Are you wanting more? This exercise will expand your thinking by taking on new ways of looking at things and opening up your perspective.

Take a moment, breathe, and think about your "What if—?" question. How could answering this question help you take the next step in bringing your brilliance forward? Experience this "What if" on a cellular level; use all of your senses. Does it feel in alignment for you? Perhaps after trying it on and discovering it's not as scary or hard as you thought, you may decide to lean in and bring your "What if" forward?

As I began to tell my story in public, afraid that they were going to judge me and be critical, I would ask myself, "What if, in fact, the audience is actually FOR me rather than against me? What if most of them are cheering for me, wanting me to succeed, just waiting to receive what I have to give?" Asking myself these questions shifted my perspective, and really helped me say yes to speaking and other opportunities.

Isn't that powerful? Think about how you can do this in your life to help you tap into your unique and wonderful brilliance. What if—? Or, What would that feel like to—? Or, Maybe I could try that? I don't have to commit to seeing myself in that identity forever and ever and ever, but what if I try it on right now?

How does that feel to you? I know for me it has changed my life. I have been able to discover talents I didn't know I had, to grow wings I didn't know could even be grown.

Your brilliance is waiting

When we see something that is broken or we don't like how it's being done, when we might think, "I know this could be different," we get frustrated; it even makes us feel stuck. But why do we just accept if? What if we could be part of the solution? What if we could really envision what it would look like, and start moving into that space? What if we could change our story? What if we could bring our gifts to the situation we are facing? What if we are *exactly* what is needed for such a time as this?

What if your experiences could help other share and shine their brilliance out into the world? What if YOU could bring forward what matters most to you?

When we have the gift to see what we want or don't want, we also have the power to see what could be different, what a possible solution could be. Seeing that gap between what is and what could be can sometimes be a horrible realization. But there's the other side of the coin: I have the power to change it, to create something better. What if I decide to do that? What would that look like? What if I want to make this difference, instead of being stuck and upset over how something is?

When things do seem wrong or we feel powerless, let's remember that we can always choose to say yes to doing something different. When we are called in this way, we don't always know the 'how,' but we will be led there if we are willing to try. Sometimes I just say, "Okay, God, I don't know what I'm supposed to do here, but I'm just going to go forward and let You do Your thing." I am never let down!

As you plant and nurture your own seeds of purpose, ask the question, "What if—?" Listen for the answer and take that step, large or small, just outside of your comfort zone—or take a major leap. Whatever that looks like for you is yours to try out, yours to do.

This is your moment and time, it's absolutely your choice. I hope you choose to say yes and welcome that next step into your brilliance. In all that you do, wherever you go, whatever may come, may you always choose to share your gifts and SHINE!

Rebecca Hall Gruyter

Rebecca Hall Gruyter (CEO of Your Purpose Driven Practice and RHG Media Productions) specializes in highlighting experts to help them reach more people around the world! From the Speaker Talent Search (that helps you find more speaking opportunities), Podcast opportunities (syndicated on multiple networks), to writing opportunities including bringing your book forward as a Best Seller.

She is an award-winning #1 International Best-Selling author multiple times over, published in over 5 magazines and over 20 books to date, plus 2 more to be released in 2019 and 3 more in 2020. A popular talk radio show host/producer, dynamic TV show host/producer, creator of the Women's Empowerment Conference Series, and an in-demand guest expert and speaker.

Rebecca has been recognized by CBS, ABC, Fox, *The Huffington Post*, *Thrive Global*, and NBC as a Top Professional in the area of Purpose Driven Entrepreneurship. With a promotional reach of over 10 million, she is committed to helping you reach more people around the world as you step into a place of influence! Remember, what the world needs is more of YOU! Rebecca wants to help you be seen, be heard, and SHINE!

Rebecca@YourPurposeDrivenPractice.com
www.facebook.com/rhallgruyter (Facebook)
www.YourPurposeDrivenPractice.com (Main Website)
www.RHGTVNetwork.com (TV Network)
www.SpeakerTalentSearch.com (Free Opportunity for Speakers to get on More Stages)
www.EmpoweringWomenTransformingLives.com (Weekly Radio Show)
www.MeetWithRebecca.com (Calendar link to schedule a time to talk with Rebecca)

Closing Thoughts

I hope you have been touched by these powerful chapters that were lovingly offered to equip and empower you to live on purpose while shining powerfully in your brilliance! All of us who have contributed to this book hope that you will continue to be encouraged on your journey and inspired to apply in your life the practical and profound tips, advice, and great wisdom that you have gleaned from this book. We can't wait to see you, hear from you, and celebrate you as you share the gift of you with the world! May you always choose to ***live on purpose and with great purpose... and SHINE in your brilliance!***

****

Books compiled or written by Rebecca Hall Gruyter to be released in 2019 and 2020:

The Animal Legacies!

This anthology featuring up to 20 authors will share heart-warming, inspiring, empowering true stories of how animals have forever touched their lives. They will share profound lessons they learned, powerful truths, encouraging messages, and a celebration and honor of their animal friends. Every reader will be encouraged, their heart touched, as each writer shares and passes on their own animal legacy. We know this book will touch your heart and your life in beautiful, empowering ways. (To be released December 2019).

The Expert and Influencers Series: Women's Empowerment Edition

This powerful anthology will feature up to 30 experts and influencers committed to inform and uplift you in the area of Women's Empowerment. From their personal and professional leadership experiences, each author will share tips, advice, and powerful insights to help you step forward as a leader in your life and business. (To be released June 2020).

Step Into Your Mission and Purpose!

This book, the second in our *Step Into* anthology series, takes the reader through the next step in their journey to SHINE! Featuring up to 30 authors, this anthology empowers readers to embrace their brilliance, and choice, to discover their unique mission and purpose in life. You will learn what it means to make the choice to live your life on purpose and with purpose. Each chapter, though the wisdom of this selection of authors, will empower and equip you to develop your own practice of living your purpose every day. Because the world needs you and your brilliance! (To be released 2021).

Anthologies Available Now That Are Compiled by Rebecca Hall Gruyter:

SHINE Series (Compiled and led by Rebecca Hall Gruyter)
- ***Come out of Hiding and SHINE!*** (Book 1 in the SHINE Series)
- ***Bloom Where You are Planted and SHINE!*** (Book 2 in the SHINE Series)
- ***Step Forward and SHINE!*** (Book 3 and final book in the SHINE Series)

Step Into Series (Compiled and led by Rebecca Hall Gruyter)
- ***Step Into Your Brilliance!*** (2019, Book 1 in the Step Into Series)
- ***Step Into Your Mission & Purpose!*** (2021, Book 2 in the Step Into Series)

Experts & Influencers Series (Compiled and led by Rebecca Hall Gruyter)
- ***Experts & Influencers Series: Leadership*** (2019, Book 1 in the Series)
- ***Experts & Influencers Series: Women's Empowerment*** (2020, Book 2 in the Series)

The Grandmother Legacies (Anthology Compiled by Rebecca Hall Gruyter)

Empowering YOU, Transforming Lives (365 Daily Inspiration Anthology Compiled by Rebecca Hall Gruyter)

Books Available Now Featuring a Chapter by Rebecca Hall Gruyter:

The 40/40 Rules Anthology compiled by Holly Porter
Becoming Outrageously Successful Anthology compiled by Dr. Anita Jackson
Catch Your Star Anthology published by THRIVE Publishing
Discover Your Destiny Anthology compiled by Denise Joy Thompson
I Am Beautiful Anthology compiled by Teresa Hawley-Howard
The Power of Our Voices, Sharing Our Story Anthology, compiled by Teresa Hawley-Howard
Succeeding Against All Odds Anthology compiled by Sandra Yancey
Success Secrets for Today's Feminine Entrepreneurs Anthology compiled by Dr. Anita Jackson
Unstoppable Woman of Purpose Anthology and workbook, compiled by Nella Chikwe
Women on a Mission Anthology compiled by Teresa Hawley-Howard
Women of Courage, Women of Destiny Anthology compiled by Dr. Anita Jackson
Women Warriors Who Make It Rock Anthology compiled by Nichole Peters
You Are Whole, Perfect, and Complete - Just As You Are Anthologycompiled by Carol Plummer and Susan Driscoll

Dear Powerful Reader,

Thank you for reading our anthology. I hope it has encouraged and empowered and uplifted you.

I wanted to share a little bit more about our organizations, Your Purpose Driven Practice™, RHG TV Network™, RHG Publishing™ and RHG Media Productions™. We are passionate about helping others live on purpose and with purpose in their life and business. I hope this book has supported and inspired you to choose to live on purpose and with great purpose in your leadership!

If you are wanting to reach more people and be part of inspiring and supporting others with your message, your gifts, and the work that you bring to the world, then I want to share some opportunities for you to consider.

Each year we compile and produce anthology book projects, support authors in publishing their own powerful books as bestsellers, produce and publish an international magazine, launch TV shows, facilitate women's empowerment conferences, get quoted in major media, launch radio and podcast shows, help experts and speakers step into a place of powerful influence to make a global difference. We provide programs and strategies to help you reach more people and facilitate the Speaker Talent Search (which helps speakers, experts, and influencers connect with more speaking opportunities). We would love to support you in reaching more people. Please take a moment to learn a little bit more about us at the sites listed below, and then reach out to us for a conversation. **We would love to help you be Seen, Heard, and SHINE!**

You can learn more about each of these things are our main website:
www.YourPurposeDrivenPractice.com
Enjoy our powerful TV and podcast shows:
www.RHGTVNetwork.com
Learn more about the Speaker Talent Search™:
www.SpeakerTalentSearch.com
Learn more about our writing opportunities:
http://yourpurposedrivenpractice.com/writing-opportunities/

If you would like to connect with me personally to explore some of our opportunities in upcoming book projects, podcast/radio shows, and/or TV, then here is the link to schedule a time to speak with me directly: www.MeetWithRebecca.com, or you can email me at: Rebecca@YourPuposeDrivenPractice.com

May you always choose to Be Seen, Heard, and SHINE!

Warmly,

Rebecca Hall Gruyter

Made in the USA
Monee, IL
24 November 2019

17372462R00085